Angry Children, Worried Parents

Seven Steps to Help Families Manage Anger

Sam Goldstein, Ph.D.
Robert Brooks, Ph.D.
Sharon K. Weiss, M.ED.

Specialty Press, Inc.
300 N.W. 70th Ave., Suite 102
Plantation, Florida 33317

Library of Congress Cataloging-in-Publication Data

Goldstein, Sam, 1952-
    Angry children, worried parents :seven steps to help families
manage anger / Sam Goldstein, Robert Brooks, Sharon K. Weiss.
    p. cm.
Includes bibliographical references and index.
ISBN 1-886941-58-0 (alk. paper)
    1. Problem children--Behavior modification. 2. Anger in children.
3. Conflict management. 4. Child rearing. 5. Parenting.
I. Brooks, Robert B. II. Title.

HQ773.G66 2004
649'.64--dc22

                                              2003058697

Edited by Jacqueline Eaton Blakley
Illustrations by Richard Dimatteo
Cover Design by Michael Wall of Kall Graphics

10 9 8 7 6 5 4 3 2 1

Printed in the United States of America

Specialty Press, Inc.
300 Northwest 70th Avenue, Suite 102
Plantation, Florida 33317
(954) 792-8100 • (800) 233-9273
www.addwarehouse.com

For Allyson, Ryan, and Janet.
S. G.

With love to Marilyn, Rich and Cybèle, Doug and Suzanne,
and Maya Kaitlyn.
R. B.

To Jack, with all my love.
S. K. W.

Thanks to Harvey C. Parker for sharing our vision and to
Kathleen Gardner for her extraordinary skill in keeping three
authors on track.
S.G.
R.B.
S.K.W.

Anger is never without a purpose, but seldom a good one.
Benjamin Franklin

We all get angry sometimes.
Fred Rogers

You will not be punished for your anger. You will be punished by your anger.
Buddha

Table of Contents

Introduction

Anger is often blamed for the problems people experience. Over the past four years it has become rare to listen to a news report, open a newspaper, or sometimes even have a discussion with neighbors without angry thoughts, feelings, and behaviors readily apparent. On many levels we are all angry about the tragic events that have taken place in the world recently, although most of us manage to contain our anger, some even channeling it into positive or at least neutral behaviors. Yet anger is reported as the primary reason for many of the negative actions of people in the world today, from young children on the playground to spouses, employees, government officials, and countries.

Because anger is increasingly prevalent in the world we have created for our children, most parents feel a sense of anxiety and trepidation when their children exhibit angry behavior resulting in family, social, or emotional problems. Most of us would prefer to live our lives without anger, but this is not possible. So we must prepare our children to understand the normal angry reactions they experience, to develop stress hardy techniques to deal with these angry emotions, and to learn effective coping behaviors to prevent anger from leading to adverse dysfunctional behavior.

Anger: A Common Problem

Even in the best functioning families children get angry—at parents, at siblings. Parents may be angry at children, and children may be angry about other issues or people outside of the home. Children become angry at parents for the same reasons they become angry at friends or teachers.

Frequently, anger is the result when a child is prevented from achieving a goal or a desired outcome. Of course, this happens in most families. Children simply can't do everything they want. When limits are set or compliance is requested, some children respond without significant outbursts or strong negative expressions of anger. Other children, however,

1

experience more difficulty managing their frustration. Thus, as with many human qualities, *the ability to respond appropriately* when goals are blocked or outcomes are not obtained varies greatly. Some children struggle significantly, often leading to an escalating pattern of conflict and anger.

When children respond well, parents often feel confident in their skills; they come to believe their child can manage anger regardless of the adversity the child faces. Yet in most of these situations parents are not quite certain what they have done that has allowed the child to respond well. Why does one child handle anger effectively while other children within the family don't respond to the same parental supports? When children struggle to cope with anger and respond in aggressive or inflexible ways, parents often feel angry, helpless, and frustrated. They are uncertain what they have done to precipitate this problem and frustrated with not knowing how to deal with it.

A Walk Down Mulberry Street
How much do we really know about anger? What role does it play in human behavior? Is it an important one? What kind of a world might we have if no one ever became angry? How much do we know about parents' and children's experiences with anger? How many families deal with angry children on a daily basis? Consider a walk down Mulberry Street.

The Kennedy Family
Michael is eleven years old. For as long as his parents can remember, he has always had a short fuse. He appears to possess a very low tolerance for stress, which often leads to angry outbursts. This pattern of behavior, which has been described by his teachers as impulsive, leads to frequent squabbles with family members and with peers on the playground and in the classroom.

Michael is trying to put together a model he has purchased with money saved from his allowance. The model is complicated, but Michael is trying to assemble it without reading the instructions. As he struggles to correctly assemble the many small pieces of this ship, he becomes increasingly frustrated. Anger floods over him, quickly displacing logical thinking. Out of frustration, in a split second Michael picks up the model and slams it to the ground.

The Reese Family

Eight-year-old Ellen has always been somewhat shy and quiet. Her parents, teachers, and coaches have noted that although she possesses many skills she doesn't appear to believe in her abilities. Ellen's teacher this year has been particularly demanding, believing that if she places more responsibility on her shoulders, Ellen will eventually recognize her competence and ability. Instead, Ellen's feelings of helplessness and hopelessness have intensified over the past six months. These feelings have increasingly led to angry outbursts. Not surprisingly, when Ellen's mother reminds her to clean up her room Ellen turns and in a loud, angry, voice, with tears filling her eyes, tells her mother, "I can't do anything right! Why won't people leave me alone? Maybe everyone would be better off if I were dead!"

The Juarez Family

Fourteen-year-old Janet finds all kinds of things to worry about, from whether the doors of the house are locked to whether her parents will arrive home safely from work. Over the past year Janet has discovered that she doesn't like these worrisome thoughts, but she has been unable to clear them from her mind. One day during a disagreement with her brother, she realized that when she was angry she didn't worry. Janet's parents have noticed over the past year an increasing pattern of angry behavior over minor events, leading to frequent family squabbles and disagreements.

The Esken Family

Nine-year-old Michelle has a learning disability. This affects her ability not only to read and write but to understand directions and express her thoughts and feelings. Her parents, unfortunately, remain unaware of the reasons for her struggles. They recognize that school is difficult for Michelle. They are becoming convinced that her lack of follow-through at home is the result of a behavioral rather than developmental problem. In response, they have decided to increase Michelle's punishment until she complies more consistently at home. Unfortunately, this intervention has not improved Michelle's ability to communicate. She has begun to feel more frustrated and angry toward her parents, feelings that typically lead to a series of tantrums that are uncharacteristic for Michelle.

The Smith Family

In the past year, the Smiths and their son, Richard, have relocated to a new city because of Mr. Smith's job. At the very same time, Mr. Smith was diagnosed with a chronic illness, which further added to the family's financial and emotional stress. Richard's parents, preoccupied with significant family matters, failed to notice his stress over the move and the loss of his best friend. Richard, usually mild mannered, lashes out at his sister in response to a minor problem, surprising the Smiths.

The Schwartz Family

Across the street, the Schwartz household is usually a hotbed of emotion. Mr. and Mrs. Schwartz were raised in homes in which anger was the primary means by which discipline was administered. In response to the model they learned, they too often use anger as a means of disciplining their children. In response, their children demonstrate similar behavior. The Schwartzes were surprised when they observed their fifteen-year-old daughter, Gail, angrily berating her younger sister over a minor problem.

The Collins Family

Seven-year-old Travis Collins was sent home from school today. Usually well behaved in class, Travis frequently experiences problems on the playground due to angry behavior. Although the principal noted that Travis had the right to be upset because he was teased by another boy for wearing glasses, Travis's angry outburst in striking the other boy and knocking him to the ground was unacceptable and resulted in a one-day suspension from school.

As these examples illustrate, children differ a great deal in their ability to cope with frustration and manage anger. Our goal in writing this book is to show parents how to teach their children important anger management skills. We all experience anger, so managing and controlling it is critical. We will suggest positive practices that parents and teachers can use to promote anger management. Based on our combined years of research and experience with many families, we have developed a practical, hands-on, seven-step program to reduce excessive anger problems and to teach all children to manage anger effectively.

Seven Steps to Managing Anger Effectively

The chapters in this book represent the seven sequential steps necessary to help children learn to manage anger. Let's preview the seven steps.

Step 1: Understand Why Children Become Angry
In the first step we explain the nature and causes of anger and explore the role it plays in everyday life. We differentiate between *being* angry and *acting* angry, a distinction that puts you in a better position to help your child learn and develop anger management strategies.

Step 2: Determine When You and Your Child Need Help
In this step we provide a set of guidelines to help you understand when anger is a problem for your child. We then give specific information to help you determine when you need professional help to teach your child anger management and offer guidelines for selecting and evaluating a professional counselor.

Step 3: Help Your Child Become an Active Participant in the Process
For anger management strategies to be effective, children must be active participants in the process of learning how to manage anger. In this step we offer a basic set of guidelines to help you nurture an optimistic mindset in your child through an empathic, destigmatizing, and demystifying approach to anger. We will provide you with strategies to teach your child about thoughts, feelings, and behaviors. A tool we call the *anger thermometer* will give you a practical way to discuss with your child how anger can

be assessed and expressed constructively. We will offer tips to help you control your anger as you teach anger management to your children. Finally, we will define and explain the role negative scripts and mindsets play in preventing individuals from effectively using the strategies they possess to manage anger.

Step 4: Employ Strategies to Manage and Express Anger Appropriately
In this step we offer a variety of strategies, including modeling, effective communication and discipline, relaxation, and problem solving, to assist in the process of anger management.

Step 5: Develop a Daily Management Plan and Put It into Action
This step provides guidelines to help you prevent anger from becoming a significant source of conflict within your family. It discusses the difference between being a reactive and responsive parent. Strategies to establish routines, facilitate parental agreement, and make life predictable are presented.

Step 6: Assess and Solve Problems
In this step we review the most common problems parents experience at home relative to angry behavior in themselves and their children. We discuss issues related to unrealistic expectations, minimizing power struggles, and knowing when it's time to "take a break."

Step 7: Instill a Resilient Mindset in Your Child
It is increasingly recognized that children are less likely to struggle with anger management if they
- feel special,
- feel appreciated for who they are,
- are capable of learning from mistakes,
- develop responsibility, compassion, and a social conscience, and
- learn competencies valued by others.

In this step we provide a set of guidelines to help you instill these qualities—considered together, we call it a *resilient mindset*—in your child.

Track Your Progress

Use this checklist to track your progress as you go through the seven steps.

_____ I understand why my child gets angry.

_____ I know how to evaluate my child's anger and determine whether my child and I require professional help.

_____ I recognize the importance of creating a working alliance with my child and have set in place a number of strategies to do so.

_____ I understand the most effective strategies to help children manage anger.

_____ I have set a plan into place to help my child manage anger and to resolve family conflict.

_____ I have carefully searched for obstacles that might reduce the effectiveness of my plan and have implemented strategies to deal with those obstacles.

_____ I understand the importance of helping my child develop a resilient mindset and have implemented five strategies to do so.

Summary

If your child experiences anger management problems, you are not alone. It is our hope that as you read this book you will find effective solutions. The strategies and ideas you will read about are based on empirical research and clinical experience. We are confident that following these seven steps will help your child develop effective anger management strategies.

When you turn the page, you will take the first step to helping your children develop effective anger management strategies. As you work through each step in this book you will move closer to an effective long-term plan for your child as well as your family.

Step 1

Understand Why Children Become Angry

What Is Anger?

Anger is a natural human emotion, one of many responses individuals can express when they are prevented from reaching their goals. Given that anger is an emotion expressed by all human beings, it seems logical to conclude that there is nothing wrong with *feeling* angry. The problem occurs when anger either consciously or unconsciously leads to inappropriate actions or behavior. The problem, then, is not being angry but choosing to deal with angry feelings in an ineffective way. How do you respond when you're angry? How did your parents respond when you were a child? Did they punish you when you expressed anger? Did they shame or blame you? Do you have a tough time dealing with anger because your parents didn't know how to deal with it? Childhood experiences powerfully influence the way parents express anger and teach their children to manage anger.

Anger can be experienced not just as an emotion but as a physical response that causes adrenaline to rush through the body, leading to agitation. Do you yell when you are angry? Do you become cynical or overreact? Do you hit your children? Although anger is a natural emotion and a potential feeling for all of us, it is a combination of experience and genetics that allows some people to manage anger better than others. It is a skill that can be modeled and taught to your children. It is this interaction of genetics and experience that ultimately determines whether children develop adaptive coping strategies to deal with anger or a pattern of dysfunctional behavior and relationships.

Remember that children don't always do what we say. They are more often likely to do what we *do*. Thus, a key component of this seven-step program is for you, the adult, to manage anger and model effective anger coping strategies for your children. Given that we accept that all of us can become angry, we choose to view anger as a signal, an indication to the individual that a goal or outcome is being blocked and that frustration is building. How children—or adults, for that matter—learn to respond to this signal will determine ultimately whether they manage anger or anger manages them. In response to anger, some blame others as the source of their problems. They use anger as fuel to drive and justify what they view as a necessary response. In this seven-step program, we help you teach your children that anger is a signal to take action rather than a sign of being treated unfairly.

What Role Does Anger Play in Everyday Life?
Anger begins as an emotion of varying intensity. It can be experienced as a mild irritation or as unbearable frustration. At the extreme end, particularly for children who are impulsive or inflexible, anger often leads to intense fury and rage. As with other emotions, anger is accompanied by physical and biological changes in the body. Heart rate and blood pressure increase. Levels of certain hormones, such as adrenaline, increase, leading to other physical changes in the body. Some researchers have suggested that aggression in response to anger may be instinctual. They suggest that anger may be a natural, adaptive response to stress, allowing people to respond to a perceived threat and defend themselves. Therefore, a certain amount of anger is likely necessary for survival, even in our complex, civilized society. But when defense occurs in the absence of true provocation, anger becomes a liability. It also becomes a liability when we react verbally or physically in an extreme way to angry feelings, when children are unable to modulate anger, or when problems occur at home, on the playground, and in the classroom.

Causes of Anger
Webster's *New World Dictionary* defines *anger* as "a feeling of displeasure resulting from injury, mistreatment, opposition, etc., usually showing itself in a desire to fight back at the supposed cause of this feeling." Anger can be

caused by external or internal events. We can become angry at other individuals, objects, or a particular situation. Sometimes we become angry about our perceptions of events or in response to how we believe we have been treated, even though our perceptions and beliefs may not be accurate.

Some children with very low emotional thresholds and intense reactions become angry over minor everyday events that rarely cause emotional discomfort for others. Conflicts with peers and siblings cause kids to become angry over issues ranging from possessions to comments made about seating arrangements in the car. Anger is a normal response to physical assault or verbal taunting or teasing. In some cases, children become angry when they are ignored or restricted from activities. Of course, all parents know that children become angry when they can't do what they want. Sometimes we are surprised by our children's angry responses in activities, such as losing a game, or to a perception that they have been treated unfairly. Those with psychiatric and emotional problems are much more prone to become angry. Children with attention deficit hyperactivity disorder (ADHD) struggle to develop self-control, so they are prone to become angry over minor, frustrating events. Anger is also a powerful emotion used by children with excessive worry or anxiety as a means of reducing worrisome feelings. In the model developed by Drs. Barbara Ingersoll and Sam Goldstein, children with depression are described as struggling due to feeling "lonely, sad, and angry." Anger appears to be a very common response when children feel helpless or hopeless. When anger overcomes us we don't think logically or rationally. As an expression of frustration, anger also fuels feelings of unhappiness.

The Three-Stage Process of Anger

Is anger like a pressure cooker? If it is a natural response to displeasure or frustration, does it always have to lead to aggression? If it builds up, does it always have to explode like a faulty pressure cooker? The answer is a resounding *no!* Almost anywhere in the three-stage process of anger—the *internal emotion,* the *external behavior,* and the *response from the environment*—outcome can change. Even during the "aftershock" of the response of the environment to an angry outburst, the experience and expression of anger can be altered.

In the first stage, as we noted, anger represents a sense of arousal usually occurring when the achievement of a goal is prevented or the fulfillment of a need is blocked. Anger is often expressed in these situations in response to the stress of the difference between the expected and actual outcome.

In the second stage of anger, individuals externalize their feelings through behavior or verbalization. With children and teens, this can include something as simple as a sour face, crying, muttering, sulking, or a random verbalization to express frustration, or as severe as physical and verbal attacks toward the source of the frustrating experience. It doesn't matter whether the frustrating experience is a conflict with a sibling, an uncooperative model airplane, or a difficult school project: the outcome is still the same. Thus, a teenager might trash the project, a child might get angry and kick his bicycle when he falls off or become angry with a friend who won't behave in a certain way and kick the friend. When anger progresses to an aggressive physical or verbal response in which the child seeks revenge as a means of retaliation, everyone ends up unhappy.

In the third stage of anger, or what we refer to as the *aftershock* of the anger volcano, the manner in which the environment responds to the child determines what happens next. If a child learns that an angry, aggressive response achieves a desired goal, that response will more likely follow every time. It is a reasonable rule of thumb that the strength of the volcano's explosion is directly related to the level of the aftershock. Children with severe problems modulating anger—that is, those who respond excessively to minor sources of stress or tension—often experience a strong sense of guilt following their angry outbursts.

We believe it is during this third stage of anger, when the consequences of the expression of anger are brought to bear, that the greatest harm occurs to a child's emerging self-esteem and sense of competence. It is within these consequences that friendships are lost, parent-child relations are threatened, and the seeds of depression are planted. Many children experience punishment or other forms of parental response to their anger that do little to provide them with the tools and skills necessary to respond to frustrating life events more effectively.

Teaching Anger Management

The goal of teaching children anger management is to reduce excessive reactions leading to anger and to develop skills to use anger as a signal to redirect behavior. As with learning to swim or ride a bicycle, as you begin to work with your child it is important to keep an open mind. Not all children learn to swim in the first lesson or master riding a bicycle the first day. Some children require much longer periods of practice to develop proficiency. Children and teens with a low emotional threshold will experience excessive reactions to anger. As we have noted, these kids anger quickly and experience more intense feelings of anger leading to excesses in behavior and action. They have a low tolerance for frustration and a high intensity of reaction. These children often require professional help. (Step 2 provides guidelines to decide when professional help is needed.)

Keep in mind also that some children are born more likely to be irritable and easily angered. These symptoms usually present from an early age. Yet it is also important to remember that some children behave this way because they live in households in which they are exposed to models of poor anger management. Some children experience both risks, leading to a significant probability that they will struggle to learn to manage anger effectively.

In part, the goal of this seven-step program is to help children and adolescents express anger in an assertive rather than aggressive manner. This means they are neither pushy nor demanding, but learn to be respectful advocates for themselves. This also means that they learn to cope with, not simply suppress, their anger. Suppression is only a partially effective strategy. When angry feelings are suppressed they often emerge later on, usually in an excessive way in response to a minor event related to an earlier anger-provoking experience. Suppressed anger is also thought to contribute to passive-aggressive behavior such as getting back at people indirectly without telling them why or confronting them directly. It also fuels cynical or hostile behavior, leading children to be excessively critical and fault-finding.

In his book for parents of severely angry children, *The Angry Child*, Dr. Tim Murphy offers suggestions to help parents defuse the anger process. We present these suggestions here to help you get started and to begin thinking in effective ways relative to your children's anger.

The First Stage: Internal Emotion

As anger builds up, avoid unnecessary frustrating situations. Recognize problems and situations that may be too difficult for your children to deal with. Establish an atmosphere of respect and caring in the home. Model effective anger management strategies and don't belittle yourself or put your children down when you are angry. Discipline with fairness and consistency and treat your children the way you would like to be treated.

When you perceive a situation as likely to spark an angry response, check for misunderstandings. Stick with the rules. Attempt to use humor. Don't let the situation get out of control. Listen, stay calm, and focus on labeling feelings correctly.

The Second Stage: External Behavior

When a child chooses an inappropriate means of expressing anger, stay in control, be respectful and reasonable, and do not resort to threats or aggression. Most important, do not get caught up in arguments. Although not all arguments are based in anger, arguments typically occur when people are angry.

The Third Stage: Response from the Environment

As your child gains control, don't ignore the problem or pretend it doesn't exist, but don't push the child to talk about the problem until you are sure she is back in control. Follow through on discipline, maintain love, practice forgiveness, and help your child develop strategies so the problem doesn't occur again.

Summary

Anger is a common human emotion. When it is used as a cue to recognize building frustration and guide alternative behavior, it can be an effective emotion. But when anger is allowed to grow unchecked it often leads to inappropriate physical and verbal behavior. By understanding the normal nature of anger, the experiences that fuel anger, and the steps leading to and following angry outbursts, you are now in a position to begin changing your behavior and helping your child.

Step 2

Determine When You and
Your Child Need Help

All children become angry at different times for different reasons, and they express this anger differently. Some children are prone to experience and express their anger more intensely than others. Some children display angry feelings in ways that are constructive and lead to a positive outcome, while others cope with their anger in a manner that magnifies their problems and leaves them even more frustrated and distressed. As they grow, most children learn to deal with their anger in appropriate ways so it does not interfere with their daily functioning. However, others continue to experience problems coping with anger into their adult lives. When it is not managed effectively, anger not only leads to poor relationships with others but also interferes with physical and emotional well-being.

Because all children become angry at times, the purpose of this chapter is to help parents identify the signs that indicate that anger in their child has become a problem and is interfering with the child's everyday life. We will also examine when professional help is indicated.

When Does Anger Become a Problem?

Parents must realize that even seemingly calm children who do not easily become upset will become angry on occasion and might even convey their anger with some intensity. When such an episode occurs it should not immediately be interpreted as a signal that anger is a problem. How frequently and rapidly children become frustrated and angry, how they cope with their angry feelings, and how they respond to attempts to calm and soothe them offer general guidelines for evaluating the extent to which the management of anger is a problem. Let's look more specifically at the questions you can raise that will help you to evaluate whether your child's anger has crossed over into a problem area.

1. Does your child quickly become upset and angry in response to many things, including some situations that objectively do not seem to warrant anger? While we cannot offer a specific number of incidents that must occur above which problems are indicated, we do know that your child is struggling with anger when verbal and physical outbursts appear on a regular basis. Parents are often aware when their child is not dealing with anger effectively.

2. Do your child's angry episodes last a long time even when you attempt to help her calm down? Does the anger tend to escalate, leading at times to a meltdown? When children cannot soothe themselves and are vulnerable to ongoing and intense bouts of anger, it is a sign that anger is not well managed.

3. Does anger keep your child from engaging in activities with other children? Children who have outbursts within their peer group are often ostracized. They receive few (or no) invitations to play, accompany friends or join activities, and their invitations for peers to come over are often met with rejection. They find themselves alone and lonely, failing to recognize how their behavior has affected their peers.

4. Is your child's schoolwork affected by frustration and anger? Some children become so frustrated with school and homework that they rip up papers, throw books on the floor, break pencils, and blame teachers for giving too much work or not explaining subject matter. Problems with school are especially evident at home when your child attempts to complete homework. Anger is problematic if school assignments consistently trigger tension and outbursts.

5. Does your child frequently damage property? Some homes literally bear the marks of a child with anger problems—holes in the wall, broken objects, doors with dents in them, words scrawled on the wall. When anger leads to vandalism and physical damage, it is a clear sign that it is out of control.

6. Does your child complain of physical ailments, yet a physical exam does not reveal any medical causes? Although such ailments might be linked to different factors, one possibility is that your child has difficulty with the expression of anger. This is especially true of children who suppress anger. For a variety of reasons they are fearful of appropriately expressing anger; instead, it finds expression in such forms as stomachaches and headaches.

7. Is it difficult to reason with your child? Does he immediately argue and say you are unfair, often screaming and shouting? Does your child respond to your requests with verbal and physical outbursts, drowning out any attempt to speak with him?

8. Does your child have difficulty when losing a game? For example, does she accuse the other person of cheating or quit when she is losing? Or, when your child wins, does she gloat and make derogatory comments about the opponent? These may all be indications of a child beset with anger and self-esteem issues.

If you have answered affirmatively to several of these questions, anger may play a significant negative role in your child's everyday life. This is particularly so if you observe signs of anger that last for more than several weeks and become increasingly intense and problematic.

Seeking Professional Help

Although our goal in this book is to teach parents specific steps to help children and adolescents deal effectively with anger, some children may require more help than their parents can provide. When this occurs, a consultation with a professional is warranted. You might consider seeking professional help for your child under the following circumstances.

- Your child's verbal and/or physical anger intensifies despite attempts both you and the child make to change this behavior.
- You or your child become increasingly frustrated or discouraged when attempting to manage these issues.
- You observe sudden behavioral changes in your child such as severe temper tantrums, irritability, or stubbornness, or a tendency to become sullen and withdrawn; your child is unable to discuss these behaviors and you cannot find a plausible cause.
- Your child is exposed to a highly traumatic event (such as being harmed or injured or enduring a natural disaster) that results in a change in behavior.
- You notice your child constantly bullying other children or siblings; your child is prone to verbal or physical assaults, often without any provocation.

Once you conclude that professional help is needed, you might wonder whom to contact. In many instances, consultation with your child's pediatrician or family doctor is a sensible first step; typically these professionals are aware of your child's developmental history and are people you trust. An initial consultation with your child's physician is especially warranted when physical symptoms such as headaches and stomachaches are present. A physician can determine whether a medical problem is associated with or contributing to the behavioral problems. If not, a physician may then refer parents to a counselor, social worker, or psychologist.

Another important source of information and assistance is your child's school. School psychologists, social workers, and counselors are trained to help, particularly if a child's difficulties with anger are displayed in school or are school related. School personnel are often knowledgeable about both public and private service providers in the area and can offer referrals to parents who seek assistance outside of the school setting.

The following are some questions to ask if you are looking for a mental health professional to work with you and your child.

1. Is the person licensed by the state in which he practices? Being licensed at least verifies that the person has a certain level of training and expertise.

2. Does the practitioner often see children and/or teens in her practice? It is important that the clinician you select has training working with this age group and parents.

3. Does the professional have adequate training to address your child's unique concerns and needs? Although some clinicians have excellent training, you want to make certain that the one you choose has experience with the kinds of problems your child is displaying.

4. Is the clinician willing to consult with your child's school (if indicated)? It is crucial that there be coordination and cooperation among the different professionals working with your child.

5. Does the person seem open and friendly? Do you sense that this is someone with whom your child will feel comfortable? What is your child's reaction when meeting the clinician? Remember that it takes some children a few meetings before feeling at ease with a therapist, but both your reaction and that of your child are indicators of how well all of you can work with this individual.

6. Does the practitioner return phone calls promptly? A complaint that is heard all too often from parents concerns therapists who take several days to return a phone call. Even busy clinicians can call for a moment and set up a time to speak further if the situation is not an emergency. Promptly returning calls indicates genuine care for you and your child.

7. After assessing your child's needs does the clinician provide feedback to you, either verbally or through written reports? If a verbal summary is provided, consider audiotaping the session with the counselor's permission for later review. Most professionals will provide a written summary of their assessment and recommendations when requested.

8. Does the practitioner enlist your input in developing and implementing a treatment plan so that you feel involved in interventions to help your child? Practitioners are consultants, and parents are case managers. It is essential that you understand your role in the treatment process, particularly in practicing and reinforcing anger management strategies with your child.

If you answer no to any of these questions, you should openly discuss those issues with the therapist. If you feel that your questions are not addressed or that your child's therapist is distant, unapproachable, or dismissive, seek help from someone else.

Keep in mind, however, that it is therapeutically appropriate for a clinician not to discuss with parents all of the information shared by children in a counseling session. It is important for therapists to maintain some degree of confidentiality with the children they treat. If you have concerns about confidentiality you should discuss them with the therapist. Children, and particularly teens, need to feel confident that the person they are confiding in is not going to convey their private thoughts to their parents, teachers, or friends. There are many reasons for this, including not wishing to be embarrassed, not wanting to worry parents, not wanting to get in trouble, or just wishing to maintain some privacy. Rest assured that even with these restrictions, therapists can effectively communicate with parents and solicit their support and participation without compromising confidentiality. They can discuss with children and adolescents when they believe sharing certain information with parents is necessary, especially when issues of safety are involved.

Once you and your child choose a therapist with whom you are comfortable, the goal is to work collaboratively to address the issues of anger. The intervention methods used may vary from one therapist to the next, but are likely to involve a combination of behavioral and cognitive strategies, some of which will be described in Step 4. Therapists may have meetings alone with the child, meetings with the parents, as well as family meetings. The goal of the meetings should be to gain information about what may be triggering a child's anger, how this anger is expressed, and what steps have been attempted in the past to manage the anger constructively; this information can then lead to a consideration of new strategies for dealing with anger.

Whatever techniques the therapist employs, parents should always be active participants in the process, following through on suggestions from the therapist. Parents are typically called on to provide coaching and encouragement outside of the therapeutic setting. Also, in order to help their child with anger management, parents must make certain that they serve as appropriate models in terms of how they express their own anger. Children are astute observers of what we do and not just what we say. Whether we wish to or not, we serve as significant models for our children. They notice if we lose our temper constantly or if we struggle to express anger constructively.

The Role of Medication in a Treatment Plan for Anger

Unlike other childhood conditions, such as attention deficit hyperactivity disorder (ADHD), oppositional defiant disorder, conduct disorder, depression, and anxiety, anger in and of itself does not constitute a clinical diagnostic category. As we have discussed, excessive anger is often a symptom of a variety of biological, emotional, and experiential problems. As such, there are no psychiatric medications marketed specifically for anger control or anger management.

However, anger management problems are often targets of medication treatment for the types of conditions just listed. Researchers report that many classes of medication, including stimulants, antidepressants, antipsychotics, and even anticonvulsants, have been reported to reduce the expression and intensity of anger in children with these conditions. If anger as a symptom is to be a target of medication treatment, it is important for you to understand how each of these different classes of medication acts, which class of medication is appropriate for which type of diagnostic problem (even though anger presents in all of them), and the benefits medicines may provide in reducing anger problems. As we have discussed, a strong tendency toward anger may also be an inherited trait that some children bring with them into the world. For this group of children, medication is necessary but likely not sufficient to provide the lifetime skills necessary to manage angry thoughts and control angry behavior. Parents should also be aware that despite many studies demonstrating the effectiveness of these medications for specific symptoms of psychiatric conditions, there are very few well-controlled studies of these medications used specifically to treat anger management. There are also some studies of individuals demonstrating extreme aggression in the face of anger in which certain classes of medication, such as anticonvulsants, have been found to reduce these severe outbursts. These are issues parents should discuss in depth with prescribing physicians.

Summary

The remaining steps in this book will teach you specific strategies to help your child deal more constructively with anger. If the source of anger remains difficult to define or if the anger becomes more frequent and more intense, the information in this and subsequent steps will help you decide when and how to seek professional assistance.

Step 3

Help Your Child Become
an Active Participant in the Process

A basic characteristic of emotional well-being and resilience is the ability
to distinguish between what we can and cannot control in our lives and to
focus our energies on those areas that are within our power to change. When
children do not handle anger effectively they often become increasingly
overwhelmed. Many children who display verbal and/or physical tantrums
feel upset by their lack of control even if they are prone to blame others for
their anger. Some are scared. One nine-year-old boy with anger problems
said, "I hate when I scream and kick things. Sometimes I get scared that I
won't be able to stop."

Nurture an Optimistic Mindset
If we want our children to deal successfully with frustration and anger, we
must reinforce an optimistic mindset, one characterized by realistic hope
and a belief that problems are surmountable. A guiding principle in helping
children to develop this mindset is to involve them as much as possible in
the process of managing, rather than being enslaved by, their feelings. The
extent and nature of the involvement will vary from one child to the next,
depending on such factors as the child's developmental and cognitive level
and the intensity of the anger; however, even a small degree of participation
can become a major force in helping children become less angry and express
anger more constructively. Let's examine some of the things you can do as
a parent to reinforce a feeling of optimism and control in your children.

Be Empathic
A crucial first step is for parents to practice empathy. As much as possible,
we must place ourselves in our children's shoes and see the world through

their eyes. In the process of helping a child deal with anger, empathic parents ask several important questions, including the following.

1. In anything I say or do with my child, what do I hope to accomplish? In a situation that involves a child's anger, one of the main goals is to help the child be less frustrated and to express anger constructively.

2. Am I saying or doing things in a way in which my child is most likely to listen to me and feel I really care? Another way of phrasing this question is, Would I want anyone to behave or speak to me the way I am behaving or speaking to my child? As an example, in response to a child's anger, many well-meaning parents attempt to ameliorate the situation by saying, "Calm down" or "There's nothing to be so angry about." However, such statements fail to validate what the child is experiencing. Many angry children would love to calm down, but they don't know how to do so. Furthermore, telling an angry child that there is no reason to be angry often evokes more anger.

Being empathic does not imply that you fail to set limits on angry behavior in your children, but that you set limits in a way that makes them more likely to listen. It involves understanding the factors that might be triggering your child's anger and analyzing whether those factors can be altered. For instance, if you know that your child becomes angry when you ask him to put his toys away, you might say, "In five minutes we have to put the toys on the shelves. Do you want to do it by yourself or do you want me to help you?" If in the past your directions to turn off the computer sent your teenager into a tirade, offer the choice of ten more minutes now or thirty more minutes additional computer time later: "It's up to you." Providing a choice often serves as a preventive measure.

3. How would I want my children to describe me when I attempt to help them deal with their anger, and how would they actually describe me? If we want our children to cooperate with us, they must sense that we understand their distress and that we are their allies, not their critics. When they voice or demonstrate anger, we must convey to them that we know kids get angry but we have to figure out the best way for them to express their anger so they don't get in trouble. If appropriate, share a story from your childhood about a time you became angry and emphasize how you learned to deal with it. If your child experiences you as empathic, he is more likely to join in the process of managing his feelings.

Destigmatize and Demystify Anger

It is difficult enough for a child to struggle with frustration and anger, but the burden is intensified when anger is accompanied by beliefs that add to a sense of distress. For instance, even youngsters who are prone to blame others for their outbursts may be concerned that their anger has made their parents unhappy or that they have disappointed their parents; some are embarrassed and believe that there is something wrong with them, that they are "crazy," while others believe that they are all alone and no one else experiences the anger and outbursts that they do.

As parents, we must become as knowledgeable as possible about our children's anger and the sources of this anger and then use this information with our children in a nonjudgmental, supportive manner. Because every child is different, demystifying and destigmatizing children's behavior requires learning their perception of what makes them angry and how they feel about the way they are acting. Thus, parents can convey to children that all youngsters get angry about different things, that some kids get more angry than others, and that there are ways of handling these feelings. It is important for children to feel that their parents will help them in a practical manner to lessen anger. It is also important for children, and essential for teenagers, to begin to feel that they are active participants in confronting their problems.

Create a Plan with Your Child

Once you and your child have made the commitment to address the issue of anger, it is time to develop a plan of action. Steps 4 and 5 will describe how to develop and implement a plan with well-defined strategies to help your child manage anger. Your particular anger management plan will differ depending on the situation, your child's age, the factors causing anger, and the way in which the anger is expressed.

For instance, if we look at two children on Mulberry Street, Michelle Esken and Gail Schwartz, different interventions are indicated. Michelle's anger is in response to both the frustration she experiences because of her learning disability and her parents' punishing her for not completing schoolwork. Her parents require assistance in understanding the nature of Michelle's learning problems and the impact these problems have on her following through with tasks. In effect, they are punishing her for behavior over which she has little, if any, control. When they become more knowledgeable about her learning style, they will be better equipped to provide support and encouragement rather than negative consequences. They can teach Michelle what she might do when she becomes frustrated instead of having tantrums. In addition, they can work more productively with Michelle's teachers to ensure that her school program is conducive to her learning.

Gail's parents also have to make changes to help Gail, but their angry behavior is more entrenched, the product of being raised in homes in which discipline was marked by anger. It is not surprising to find that Gail yells at her younger sister; in fact, she is modeling her parents' disciplinary style. Family counseling sessions are indicated as a means for the parents to examine their pattern of discipline and behavior and the ways in which all family members relate with each other. This examination will be necessary to develop a more positive and less punitive family climate.

To begin the process of evaluating, identifying, and addressing factors that increase anger in your child requires basic information about life at home, in the community, and at school. Have your child consider the questions in the Anger Worksheet on page 29 to help you begin this process.

Help your child answer the questions and provide input with your own observations in a nonaccusatory way. Encourage your child to return the worksheet once he's completed it on his own. Make sure he knows that every family member will do so as well. Then answer these same questions in terms of your own behavior.

Anger Worksheet

Ask your child the following questions in order to get useful information about his or her daily life and anger management techniques.

1. Think of the last two times you were angry. What was happening?

2. Do your angry feelings come suddenly or can you tell when they are beginning?

3. When you get angry, where do you feel it in your body?

4. Think of a time you got angry. What did you do? How did you handle your anger?

5. What happened after you displayed your anger?

6. Could you think of other ways to display your anger?

7. Can you think of one time you were happy with the way you expressed your anger?

8. Do you ever hold your anger in and try not to show it?

9. Why would you try not to show it? What do you think might happen?

Teach Your Child About Thoughts, Feelings, and Behaviors

This process is closely related to the process of demystifying fears and anxieties for your child. It can be beneficial for your child to understand how our thoughts and feelings influence our behavior. Obviously, the explanation offered must be in keeping with your child's cognitive and developmental level. For example, consider a ten-year-old boy we worked with who had learning disabilities and who began each day in school by hitting another child. At home, when doing his homework, he shouted that his teacher didn't know how to teach and that the work was dumb. As he struggled to complete his assignments, he became increasingly upset and would often rip up papers and throw things.

It was helpful for this boy to learn that engaging in schoolwork assaulted his sense of competence and elicited angry feelings and thoughts, prompting him to blame others so as to avoid feeling further humiliation. He also resorted to angry behavior as a means of expressing his frustration.

In our interventions, we said we could try to figure out several things, including what made him angry, what he thought about when he became angry, and how he handled these feelings (that is, what were his coping behaviors). Casting the issue in this way helped him to gain greater control of the problem. He demonstrated exceptional insight when he said, "I think I know why I used to hit other kids at school. I'd rather hit another kid and be sent to the principal's office than have to be in the classroom where I felt like a dummy." This boy's anger was not only in response to his frustration when confronted with learning tasks, but was also used as a coping technique to remove him from the classroom. Unfortunately, this coping behavior worsened rather than improved his situation.

Given his new understanding of how feelings, thoughts, and behaviors interacted, he "caught himself" when frustration set in and learned to challenge the assumption that he was "dumb." This new perspective permitted him to develop more productive ways of coping, such as requesting additional help from the teacher. Also, as the teacher learned more about his learning strengths and vulnerabilities, she was able to modify his assignments in keeping with his needs. These accommodations further reduced his frustration and anger.

An adolescent acting disrespectful with teachers and mocking the "smart kids" may share the same issues. As a teen, she is more concerned with saving face. Understanding her learning strengths and challenges needs to be paired with comfortable ways to seek and receive assistance.

Use an Anger Thermometer

One technique for helping youngsters learn about feelings, thoughts, and behaviors and deal more effectively with anger is to represent the frequency and intensity of their anger in a visual, concrete form that we call an *anger thermometer.* The very act of "concretizing" anger may actually render these problems more manageable and less overpowering. One nine-year-old girl who created an anger thermometer said, "Now that I can see what gets me angry and how angry I get, I feel I can learn to calm down." Using the anger thermometer can increase a child's sense of empowerment and control.

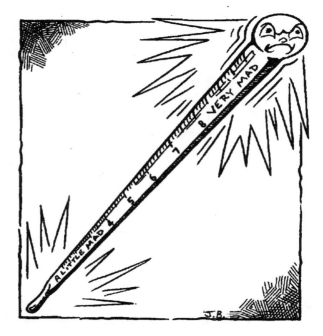

In addition, an anger thermometer can provide children with a technique for monitoring and observing their progress and then making necessary changes in their intervention program. It is often difficult to assess one's progress on a day-to-day basis, but with the assistance of an anger thermometer children can gain a longer-term perspective of change.

To introduce the anger thermometer, explain to your child that one way to control anger and to tell whether that ability is improving is to "measure" anger just as meteorologists measure temperature. With your child's input, list the two or three things that evoke anger in your child and then draw a thermometer with numbers from 1 (representing low anger) through 10 (high anger). Although some children may not know initially where to rank their anger, you can assist by listing something that causes your child a great deal of anger (for example, not being allowed to stay up after bedtime or striking out in a Little League game) and something that does not (such as the local professional baseball team losing).

As you develop and implement a plan of action to deal with the anger, you can assess with your child how things are progressing by graphing her ratings or using the thermometer every few days. This representation offers a vehicle for helping a child to observe progress, to feel more hopeful, and to become a more active participant in the process of change.

A similar tool can be used with teenagers to help them (and their parents) take a look at past blow-ups and their outcomes. Make a list of the last few situations that sparked a disagreement. Using a scale of 1 to 10, first evaluate the level of anger (10 being the most angry), then evaluate the outcome (10 being the best outcome). What often becomes evident is that the higher the anger rating, the lower the rating of satisfaction. Follow up with a list of the behaviors of both parent and child in each situation and alternative behaviors that could have been used. It is possible that the same behavior may be suitable in many situations. Try to incorporate your teen's suggested behaviors on your list of preferred responses to be used when a difference of opinion arises. Make using the scale a routine part of discussion. The usual process of bringing up behavior only when it is a problem does little to improve skills or outcome. Even a log is a simple tool that helps document situations and options so you and your child can measure progress.

It is rarely a good idea to review options at the moment of crisis. Your child is not listening and neither are you. Your teen tells you that "You never listen," and he may be correct. But a tool that provides the opportunity for objective review of feelings and behaviors in retrospect has a better chance to influence on how anger is managed in future situations.

Teach Your Child How to Solve Problems

As is evident from the examples we have offered, an optimistic mindset is rooted in children believing that there are adults who can help them to help themselves. When we demystify problems, when we teach children about the connections among feelings, thoughts, and behaviors and about how one can begin to change all three domains, and when we create ways to represent and manage anger, we are establishing the foundation necessary for the emergence of an optimistic mindset. To reinforce this optimistic mindset we must engage our children in the process of solving problems.

In order to develop strategies to manage a problem, there must be an agreement with your child that a problem exists. This is more challenging than it may seem because many children and adolescents minimize problems they have with anger and are quick to blame others for their angry outbursts. In such instances, parents must practice empathy and not attempt to extract a "confession" from their son or daughter. For instance, if a child does not accept ownership for a tirade, but instead shouts at his parents that he got angry because they wouldn't let him go out on a school night, parents can validate what he is saying. Validation does not mean they agree, but that they "hear" him.

In this situation the parents could say, "We know you get angry when we don't let you have time with your friends. We've explained the importance of school. Going out on weeknights interferes with your schoolwork and makes you too tired the next morning. When you get angry, it doesn't help to scream and shout. That doesn't solve anything." Some teens may respond, "I wouldn't have to scream or shout if you let me go out." The parents can calmly respond (we know it's not easy to be calm under these circumstances), "It's your choice how you behave when our guidelines mean you don't do something you want to do. When you choose to go on a tirade it doesn't really help. Things are said and you end up getting punished. We think you can learn to choose better ways." This last statement sets the tone to develop the kinds of strategies discussed in Step 4.

As Myrna Shure has highlighted through her "I Can Problem Solve" program in her books *Raising a Thinking Child* and *Raising a Thinking Preteen*, children even as young as preschool age can be engaged in the process of problem solving. We can ask children to reflect on several possible solutions to a problem and choose which one they think will work best. It is encouraging to observe the number of children who arrive at effective strategies.

Because children struggling with anger are prone to externalize their problems and thus have a negative attitude about interventions that involve their active participation being successful, parents can emphasize that if the first strategy that is selected doesn't work, then the child can rely on the second or third strategy. The message to our children should be that anger is a natural feeling but can become a problem if not expressed constructively, that there are steps that can be taken for the child to manage anger more effectively, that some solutions may take time to be successful, that some may not be effective at all, and that if that is the case, others will be attempted. We want to develop realistic optimism and a sense of hope in our children.

Change Negative Scripts and Mindsets

The process of considering and using new strategies to replace plans that have proved ineffective in the past demands that we as parents demonstrate the insight and courage to change our behaviors so that our children might change theirs. To use the same ineffective script repeatedly will guarantee continued frustration and anxiety. If adolescence is part of the equation there is the element of your child needing to assert his independence. Individuating from his parents is part of the job description at this age. How else can he prove himself to be different than by taking exception to almost anything his parents say? Isn't it enough for parents to deal with emerging and full-blown adolescence without the high drama and anger? Parents who have had to contend with an angry child over the years are often exhausted by the time their child is a teenager. They have less patience, as each incident culminates into the inevitable outburst. They can predict it but can't stop it.

The words and behaviors we use with our children again and again in similar situations and in similar ways become the scripts of parenting. Negative scripts often become the mainstay of many well-meaning parents' efforts to help their children overcome problems. Negative scripts contain words and actions that tend to increase family conflict and often fuel anger in all involved. But when our words and actions have positive outcomes, we can think of these scripts as being effective. They deserve to be repeated.

Robert is a four-year-old boy with difficult bedtime behavior. When it was time for bed, Robert would run through the house; when his parents attempted to restrain him, he would scream and yell. They viewed his angry behavior, which had been occurring for more than six months, as oppositional, and out of frustration they resorted to yelling at and/or spanking him. In effect, they were unknowingly contributing to his distress and outbursts. They were trapped in a negative script.

When we met Robert we saw him more as a frightened rather than an oppositional child. We felt that his angry outbursts were a reflection of anxiety. We asked him during our interview if he ever had "scary dreams." He looked surprised and said, "How did you know?" We answered that many children his age have nightmares and we wondered if he did. He said he did and actually appeared relieved to speak to us about these dreams, the main ones involving monsters pursuing him and his family. Because it is frequently helpful for children to represent or concretize their fears, we asked him to draw a picture of the monsters that we could show his parents.

Robert drew the picture and mentioned that he was afraid to go to sleep because he would then have those "bad" dreams. Although Robert's parents had originally seen his bedtime tantrums as manipulative and oppositional, we understood this behavior as a way of coping—that is, as an attempt to avoid the anxiety associated with nightmares. We discussed this alternative explanation of Robert's behavior, which elicited greater empathy on the part of his parents and prompted them to change their script.

Robert's parents were also encouraged to involve their son as an active participant in arriving at possible solutions to ease his anxiety and change his angry behavior. Much to their surprise, Robert offered two suggestions. The first was to have a nightlight, which his parents had previously refused, believing that he was old enough not to need one. The second involved a truly creative strategy, having a photo of his parents placed by his bed that he could look at when he became frightened. The parents agreed to both requests. Robert's tantrums and resistance to going to bed ended. A negative cycle was replaced with a positive script in which Robert's problem-solving skills, his sense of control, and his resilience were reinforced. By adopting a problem-solving approach, questioning negative scripts, and managing emotions, parents can usually find effective solutions to seemingly impossible problems.

Summary

It is not easy for parents to deal with ongoing tantrums and outbursts in their children. One father observed that he was "constantly poised for attack" from his fourteen-year-old daughter. He added, "I don't look forward to being with her. She loses her temper over anything. She always feels that things are not fair. Even though I tell myself not to do so, I find that eventually I lose my temper and say things I regret. I don't know how often I've told her to stop being so angry, that she ruins things for the entire family."

One can certainly appreciate this father's frustration. Even those parents who are well-intentioned may fall into the negative scripts of yelling at their children, telling their children what to do, not involving them in the problem-solving process, and becoming frustrated and angry when attempts to ease the problem are unsuccessful. If we remain empathic and remember that children will be more willing to change their behavior when they sense our support and when they feel they have some control of the situation, then we can more effectively help our children handle their frustration and anger; in the process we also nurture their confidence and self-reliance.

Step 4

Employ Strategies to Manage and Express Anger Appropriately

There are acceptable and unacceptable ways of dealing with anger. It is important to reinforce for your children that anger is a normal human emotion. Anger itself is not necessarily a problem; rather, expressing anger inappropriately is the problem. The solution is to learn to resolve angry feelings through functional actions directed toward the source of anger.

In this step we review a number of effective strategies to help you help your children reduce angry outbursts in the face of frustration, deal appropriately when angry feelings arise, express anger reasonably, and, most important, maintain a focus on the source of anger, continuing to work toward an acceptable resolution of the problem.

Set a Good Example

One of the most important and effective ways you can help your child develop positive habits is to develop and practice them yourself. Children do as you do, not as you say, so make it a priority to be the kind of person you want them to be.

Anger clouds effective communication. Imagine being equipped with a sort of autopilot that could take over when you become angry or upset with your child, guiding you to use your most sophisticated communication and anger management skills to defuse negative emotions and search for reasonable solutions. Not only would this pattern of behavior serve as a positive model for your children, but it might also minimize power struggles.

Unfortunately, it is precisely when we are angry and frustrated that our ability to locate appropriate strategies and communicate effectively is noticeably weakened. When we are angry, we often lack empathy, and our problem-solving skills become less effective. The style of angry communication that results often exacerbates rather than ameliorates a problem situation.

For example, Mr. Stanton was angry with his supervisor at work because he thought that his supervisor was being overly critical of a proposal Mr. Stanton had submitted for a new project. Fueling the anger was Mr. Stanton's feeling that his supervisor was not giving him the credit he deserved and that a negative evaluation could cost him a possible merit raise in pay.

Mr. Stanton brought his anger home. He screamed about his supervisor in front of his wife and children. He then yelled at his wife because she hadn't picked up his clothes at the dry cleaner, accusing her of "always forgetting to do things." When his 13-year-old son gave him a warning slip from one of his teachers, Mr. Stanton yelled, "You are always irresponsible! You don't take anything seriously. You never clean your room. I'm not thrilled with your friends. You are grounded for a month!"

What could Mr. Stanton have done at home? He might have considered other ways of dealing with his frustration, such as discussing his distress and anger with his wife, using relaxation techniques, or engaging in physical exercise. Doing any of these might have helped to lessen his anger and resulted in his becoming more empathic with his wife and son, thereby helping him serve as a model of managing anger effectively.

Treat Your Children As You Would Like to Be Treated

Our relationships with our children must be able to bear the stress of an angry experience or outburst. If we want and expect our children to treat us with respect, communicate clearly, and respond fairly, we have to treat them the way we ourselves would like to be treated. It can be quite difficult to control our own negative emotions and actions in the heat of the moment, but doing so can increase the probability of successfully dealing with angry situations. Listening empathically and engaging our children in discussion creates an atmosphere in which a problem-solving approach can thrive. (See Step 3 for more about being empathic.)

Discipline Effectively

One of the most important responsibilities that a parent has is to be a disciplinarian. The words *discipline* and *disciple* are derived from the same root, indicating that discipline is a teaching process, not one of intimidation or humiliation. Children feel secure in homes in which there are fair and reasonable rules and limits. We want children to learn from us, not resent us. Discipline, if applied appropriately, can lessen anger and aggression. However, if discipline is overly punitive, arbitrary, or inconsistent, it can actually intensify a child's anger. Following are guidelines for effective use of disciplinary strategies.

Provide Rewards and Incentives

Typically, behavior that is rewarded is repeated, and behavior that is punished is stopped. But it can be difficult to apply this parenting principle when dealing with a child in the midst of an angry outburst. It's only natural that these displays usually draw our attention and result in punishment. Yet when our children manage their anger effectively, respond respectfully, and communicate effectively, we may not always take notice and reward their behavior.

Take the time to notice when your children manage anger effectively. A positive comment or a kind word in this context goes a long way in helping children create the motivation necessary to manage their anger in stressful situations. A note describing the positive behavior documents your feelings. For some children, a consistent system of rewards and punishments is essential as they learn to manage anger; others seemingly master their angry reactions with ease, requiring only periodic feedback. Finding the appropriate level of consequences, both rewards and punishments, is a key component in helping your children develop effective anger management skills. As we noted in Step 3, if children are prone to angry outbursts, parents can engage them not only in devising strategies for managing anger, but also in defining consequences for both the successful and unsuccessful expression of anger.

Follow Predetermined, Flexible Rules and Limits

When rules and limits are set, it is important to stick with them consistently. It is not acceptable for children to badger or manipulate parents when they are unhappy with parental decisions. Avoid the negative script of giving in to children when they challenge reasonable expectations and consequences. Acquiescing to their demands in such situations, particularly when anger is expressed, establishes a self-centered and irresponsible mindset—exactly the opposite of the resilient mindset we want to help children develop.

Being consistent does not mean being rigid or continuing to resort to ineffective rules and disciplinary practices. When a conflict over limits and consequences has existed for a long time, and when children experience parents as nagging, lecturing, or being unfair, anger in all parties will grow. In such situations, parental words begin to fall on the proverbial deaf ears. When resentment rather than learning pervades the home atmosphere, anger is often poorly managed by all parties.

Although you must establish clearly defined, nonnegotiable rules at home even in the face of your child's anger, especially those related to safety and security, modifying rules and limits does not represent an abandonment of parental responsibility. Rules should be altered when they have become part of an ineffective negative script. Replace ineffective rules with those that are guided by the goals of lessening anger and resentment, enhancing your relationship with your children, and encouraging them to change their behavior because you are willing to change yours. You risk spoiling children only when you do away with expectations and allow children to do whatever they want.

If you find yourself modifying almost every rule and expectation you have established, especially in the face of your children's anger, consider whether your initial decisions require more thought before they are put into practice. Do you generate rules and limits primarily when you are angry or frustrated? In the heat of the moment such directives are likely to be arbitrary or harsh. Important decisions about limits and expectations are better handled when you are calm and thinking clearly.

Anticipate Problems
As the saying goes, an ounce of prevention is worth a pound of cure. It is typically easier to deal effectively with a problem when strategies are set in motion as the problem is first developing or before it develops.

Think prevention; plan ahead. Try to anticipate situations in which your child may become angry and consider how you will respond. Even better, discuss these potential conflicts with your child and talk about what you will do or how you hope she will respond. If you find yourself constantly reacting to your children's anger, you will not only fail to reduce angry outbursts but might even perpetuate future angry episodes.

Avoid Negative Models

If your children are impressionable, watch out for negative models, such as those seen on television, in the movies, or in other media. Children are spending an increasing amount of time in front of television screens. They watch television or DVDs, surf the Internet, send instant messages, and play video games. Although many children do a good job of self-selecting activities that are not likely to cause stress, other children seem incapable of doing so. In these situations, appropriate supervision of children's exposure to the media is strongly recommended.

When you set limits on media and Internet exposure, anticipate that angry children may initially become more angry. You must not only explain to your child that certain content is not appropriate for children and adolescents, but also offer alternative choices to help defuse the situation. For example, you might tell your child he can't watch a certain horror movie, but give him three other choices of movies he may watch. Although children are not likely to thank parents for these choices, in time they will probably respond positively because choices provide a sense of ownership.

In some instances, parents may have to set limits about their children interacting with others who are poor models of anger management. This might be another child in the neighborhood, or even a relative. If parents do restrict contact with particular people, they should explain why to the child at a level she can understand.

Use Timeout Effectively
Timeout is one of the most popular forms of parental discipline. It is often meted out when children become angry—or even when parents become angry in reaction to their children's behavior. Although positive forms of discipline, such as rewarding appropriate behavior, are certainly preferable, appropriately used punishments like timeouts are a very effective way to correct noncompliant behavior.

Timeout is not a direct intervention for anger, or even a tool for teaching effective anger management. Rather, it is a tactic to defuse anger in the presence of noncompliance. The purpose is not to make children feel bad or make parents feel better; it is to let a child know when she is noncompliant and give her the opportunity to get back in control and make another attempt at compliance.

In *SOS: Help for Parents,* author and psychologist Dr. Lynn Clark offers parents an extensive set of ideas and strategies for using timeout effectively. Dr. Clark notes that timeout has many advantages. It quickly weakens many types of adverse behaviors, gives children the opportunity to calm down, is fairly simple for parents to learn and use, provides parents a rational and nonaggressive means of dealing with childhood problems, is usually not time consuming, and can be adapted for use with children of different ages (although generally it is effective for children between the ages of four and twelve years).

Timeout is not *always* appropriate or advantageous. It is not a useful strategy for children who lack certain skills. For example, if a child is hyperactive and has difficulty staying seated at the dinner table, sending the child to her room doesn't really address the problem. If anything, it can result in more anger. It might prove more effective to permit the child to get up once or twice from the table as long as she is not disruptive. And keep in mind that sending a child to her room might allow her to watch television, play video games, or engage in other fun activities. If a timeout is "fun" for the child, the punishing effect is diminished or lost.

Let's consider an example of a disciplinary situation in which timeout can be used appropriately. Suppose you direct your child to take his feet off the coffee table and place them on the floor while watching television. You have reminded him a number of times, yet each time you return to the room his feet are on the table. When you indicate that if he does not keep his feet on the floor he will be restricted from television, he responds with an angry comment. In this case, a timeout is appropriate.

Sending your child to timeout is a simple procedure. Calmly state to the child that because he has not responded to your request and has become angry, he is to sit in a chair for a specific period of time ("Since you keep yelling and won't calm down when I ask you to pick up your toys, you need to sit in the chair for a minute to calm down; the minute doesn't start until you stop yelling"). You must help your child make the connection between his behavior and the timeout. Clearly state the reason for the timeout, as well as your expectations for compliance. When the time period is up, quickly bring the child back to the problem situation and again request that he comply ("I would like you to pick up your toys; it would be really helpful"). When the child returns and complies, provide positive reinforcement. If the problem arises again quickly, do not impulsively respond with annoyance, sarcasm, or anger, which only models the very behavior you seek to extinguish in your children. Respond with a clear direction and be willing to provide timeout as needed.

The timeout chair can be in the same room as the offense—preferably facing a wall or a corner, and certainly not facing the television. For young children, it can be a towel in the corner of the room. The only requirement is that the child's bottom remain in the chair or that he remain on the towel (a timeout towel is easily transported for use in other places). A child may cry or talk to himself, but he may not do anything entertaining such as playing with toys, talking to others, watching television, or listening to music.

The timeout period should be brief—as short as one minute. This is such a short amount of time that even the most restless child can easily comply. This time allows the child to return quickly to the problem situation and again attempt compliance. If the child continues to be angry and frustrated, you can send him to sit in a chair in another room until he is calm for a period of a minute; then he may return to the situation.

Guidelines for Timeout

The timeout procedure puts space between parent and child and between the child and anything that might perpetuate the behavior.

- Timeout should be in a quiet area, away from family "traffic," with no access to TV or computer. It can be on a mat or a towel, in a chair, or in a separate room.
- In a matter-of-fact tone, state the behavior, remind the child of the rule that was broken, then say "timeout." No discussion until after the timeout, if then.
- The rule of thumb is that the length of timeout is based on age. A short timeout for a five-year-old is five minutes. His long timeout may be ten minutes. Once he is in the timout area, set the timer.
- Set timer for one minute to allow time for the child to go to the timeout spot. If he is there before the time goes off, he owes a short timeout. If not, he owes a longer one.
- Timeout is over when the timer goes off, not before.

Timeout troubleshooting. Many parents become frustrated when their children refuse to go to or remain in timeout. Psychologist and author Dr. Tom Phelan, in his book *1-2-3 Magic,* describes the six kinds of behavior children exhibit to test parents' decisions, including those concerning timeout. Many of these behaviors find their roots in anger. It is helpful for parents to recognize when children engage in these behaviors and understand that they are designed to get parents to back off.

The six behaviors are as follows:
- Badgering ("Why can't I?" "Please?" "When?")
- Intimidating (banging on doors, yelling, throwing objects)
- Threatening ("I won't talk to you again!" "I'm going to run away from home!")
- Playing the martyr (crying, pouting, looking sad or depressed)
- Acting overtly sweet or nice (not usually a consequence of anger)
- Physical actions (attacking parents or physically running away)

If your child refuses to go to timeout or attempts to change the subject by throwing a tantrum or engaging in other testing behaviors, establish a process that shortens the time if she goes on her own. Explained in advance, it can be that you set a timer for one minute. If she gets to the designated place for serving timeout before the timer rings, she owes a short timeout (for example, five minutes). If she's not in timeout when the one-minute bell rings, she owes a long one (for example, ten minutes). If she refuses to go to timeout, she will have no family privileges until she serves the timeout. That means no screen time (anything that uses a screen—TV, videos, computer, video games, Internet, and so on), no snacks or sweets, no outside play, no friends in the house—none of the big stuff you can readily control. Once in timeout, set the timer for the predetermined time— one minute per year of age is a good guideline for young children. When it rings, calmly tell her time is up. No lectures, nagging, or sermonizing allowed.

Otherwise, try not reacting. Don't pay attention to her. Many parents ignore. They ignore the good, the bad, and just about everything else their children do. Ignoring is an *active* process. To ignore effectively, you must not pay attention to behavior you dislike, but immediately pay positive attention when your child begins to behave appropriately. In most situations, however, once you make a direct request of a child and she is noncompliant, ignoring will not be effective.

1-2-3 Magic

The *1-2-3 magic method* developed by Dr. Tom Phelan doesn't involve nagging or threats and helps parents avoid power struggles and arguments. When a child becomes angry, parents warn the child of the behavior and direct the child what to do instead, stating the consequence of noncompliance. When adverse behavior continues, parents hold up one finger and say to the child, "That's one." The parents then restate what they wish the child to stop and what positive action the child should take. If the child does not comply after ten to fifteen seconds, parents then hold up two fingers and say, "That's two." If the behavior persists, parents then say, "That's three" and send the child to timeout. Remember that when some children become angry their ability to rationally respond to limits is lost. Preferably, the 1-2-3 magic strategy should be used *before* children lose control.

When you request that your child follow through with a punishment such as a timeout and the child tries to manipulate by throwing an angry tantrum, your request provides the child with a clear message that you will not deal with her when she is behaving inappropriately. *When your child regains control,* return to the situation, reinforce her for being in control, and again direct her to follow through with the punishment. This is a battle your child cannot win. Although some children may repeatedly test, most quickly recognize that sooner or later they will have to go to timeout. If your child is still noncompliant the third time you return, warn the child that another punishment, such as an earlier bedtime or a television restriction, will result if she does not go to timeout on the next request. Rarely will a child continue to be noncompliant when parents patiently add additional punishments.

We do not recommend dragging children to timeout or restraining them in a timeout chair. If you physically restrain your child as a punishment, your child will place the blame on you and not on his behavior. If, on the other hand, your child is sitting voluntarily in the timeout chair, working to gain control over his anger, the child's willingness to comply is an acknowledgment of inappropriate behavior, and the chances that punishment will be effective increase.

A counting procedure gives your child a limited time to change his behavior before he incurs the consequences. With a structured (and unvarying) counting procedure, your children know how long thay have to shape up—or else—and they know what that "or else" will be. For example, give your child until the count of three to stop arguing or she has to go to her room for five minutes or give your children until the count of three to stop bickering or they must go to separate parts of the house for fifteen minutes.

It is important to reward your child for not reaching the final number. That balances out the counting, especially on rough days when it feels like all you do is count. If your final number is three, by rewarding your child for going a period of time without reaching it, getting that reward eventually becomes the motivator for stopping at two (or one).

Counting has numerous benefits as a technique for interrupting negative behavior. Because it is so simple, anyone can do it. With only a brief explanation, your child easily understands it. Moreover, any approach that makes your response predictable will seem more reasonable to your child, and, therefore, less likely to provoke an angry response. Since punishment is most effective with a minimum of discussion, counting encourages less talk and your use of that all-important matter-of-fact tone.

A more age-appropriate form of timeout for teens is grounding. Like timeout, it requires advance explanation as well as some documentation. Develop a list of five household jobs. Determine what number of chores is assigned to a specific infraction. Examples of chores include washing the kitchen floor or cleaning all tubs and showers. Each job should be written on a card, including a detailed description of what is required to complete the job correctly. For example:

Wash the kitchen floor.
1. Sweep the floor clean.
2. Remove all movable pieces of furniture.
3. Fill a bucket with warm, soapy water; wash the floor with a clean rag, squeezed dry.
4. Dry the floor with a clean, dry rag. Replace the furniture that was moved.

Explain to your child that when certain rules are broken, or following an outburst, one or more job cards will be assigned. The child will randomly select the assigned number of cards from the prewritten job cards. Until the assigned number of jobs described on the cards is completed correctly, she will be grounded.

Being grounded means there are no household privileges or social activites for a specified period of time (for example, two days) *and* until the chores are completed. The punishment is predetermined and is not up for discussion. Nor is sermonizing part of the punishment. When the jobs are completed, check to be sure that they have been done correctly. Acknowledge your child's success in completing the chores correctly, thus ending the grounding. If a job is not completed correctly, refer to the card, letting the description act as the feedback on parts done correctly or incorrectly. If the time period is over and the chores are done as specified, the grounding is complete. Your child determines how long she is to be grounded.

Remember that punishment is rarely well received. The measure of whether it is effective is that your child follows the rules more often and the angry outbursts are diminished.

Broken Record

Educator and author Rick Lavoie describes a very simple and effective strategy he calls the *broken record technique* for dealing with angry, argumentative children. This strategy is effective when the child persists in trying to start an argument. In the broken record technique, each time the child objects to a parent request, the parent softly, firmly, and calmly repeats the rule or policy as many times as needed without engaging in a discussion. Lavoie suggests that in most instances, parents will not need to repeat their request more than three times before the child or teen stops raising objections and complies with parental requests without an upsetting and unfruitful argument. The broken record technique is particularly effective in nonnegotiable situations.

Practice Effective Problem Solving

Problem solving is a multistep process that can reduce the probability of angry outbursts and is critical in finding solutions to manage excessive anger. Effective problem solving consists of four key steps.

1. Define the Problem and Agree That It Is a Problem

If a problem exists but is not clearly defined and is not acknowledged by your child, then all of your exhortations to arrive at solutions will fall on deaf ears.

Too often we misinterpret problems when we rely on our own assumptions and perceptions as being true. For example, shy, quiet, eight-year-old Ellen Reese struck out at her mother when her mother reminded her to clean up her room. Ellen's anger was the result of feeling inadequate and criticized. Yet from her mother's perspective, Ellen's response seemed to be an unprovoked, aggressive attack.

The ways in which we understand our child's problems will play a significant role in how we respond. If we experience a child as being willful, manipulative, out to get us, lazy, or a quitter, we are more likely to respond to his anger with anger and resort to behavior that will only fuel the problem. If we possess a better sense of the basis of the problem, if we recognize that some problems are predicated on a child's temperament or abilities while other problems represent the child's attempts to deal with stress or pressure, our capacity for empathy and for engaging the child in effective problem-solving strategies will be enhanced.

As part of defining a problem, you and your child must agree that there is a problem. In dealing with anger, it is rare that parents and children don't agree that there is a problem. What they don't as often agree on is the source and nature of the problem. Remember fourteen-year-old Janet Juarez, who worried excessively? Janet's problem was her inability to stop worrying and her use of anger as a means of distracting herself from worry. From her parents' perspective, Janet's problem was simply anger.

2. Consider Two or Three Possible Solutions
Defining and agreeing on the problem leads naturally to the next step, finding possible solutions. You can engage children and teens in this task by speculating about various courses of action. As much as possible, encourage your child to generate solutions, and be cautious to not dismiss any suggestion unless it goes against a nonnegotiable family rule.

The Eskens used this strategy with nine-year-old Michelle, who had a learning disability. Her angry outbursts were the result of her frustration combined with her parents' punishment, an intervention that wasn't likely to improve Michelle's self-confidence or achievement. Michelle first suggested that her mother write a note to the teacher that would excuse her from homework. Mrs. Esken explained to Michelle that homework was an important part of school and that homework helped children develop independent learning skills. Therefore, not doing homework wasn't an option.

Once you have considered a number of solutions and their possible outcomes, pick one that appears to be the best. This may not be an easy process. Unless you have a very strong reason not to, allow your child to take the lead in picking the first solution. For example, if Michelle offered to get up an hour earlier each morning to do her homework but her mother knew that Michelle had difficulty getting up on time, Mrs. Esken could say, "Getting up early to do homework is one idea, but because you like to sleep as late as possible, you probably can think of a better solution." By stating her concern in this way, Mrs. Esken promotes a nonjudgmental, problem-solving approach.

3. Develop Reminders
Most children struggling with anger—or any problem, for that matter—

feel that their parents are "nags." Even when families arrive at solutions to problems and everyone agrees to participate, there can be lapses. Family members may forget what they agreed on or make excuses for why they didn't follow through.

One of the best remedies for forgetting is to establish a strategy to remind each other to follow through on an agreed-on plan. Once you decide on a plan to handle an anger problem, tell your children, "This sounds great, but because we are human and we may forget what we agreed on, how can we remind each other so that we are not nagging?" Posting the list of solutions and using it is a good start. When children offer suggestions as to how they would like to be reminded, the probability that they will complain they are being nagged is reduced.

4. Anticipate Obstacles
Similar to the importance of insuring follow-through is to plan for possible obstacles to the success of your strategy. In this way, when potential trouble spots are defined, you are better prepared to avoid them, deal with them if necessary, or switch to a backup plan.

We have learned the value of anticipating possible roadblocks to success from experiences in our work with families. We discovered that what appeared to be sound strategies in our offices were not always effective in practice. We also found that when parents and children attempted strategies that they helped to design and the strategies didn't work, the family often felt more defeated and less disposed to attempt other interventions. However, because they considered possible roadblocks in advance, they were always confident that if a strategy proved ineffective another was waiting in the wings.

Use Relaxation Techniques
Anger affects thoughts, feelings, behaviors, and bodily responses. A number of strategies can effectively reduce anger, including breathing techniques, progressive relaxation, and imagery. We first wrote about these strategies with our colleague, Dr. Kristy Hagar, in our book *Seven Steps to Help Your Children Worry Less*. Although we originally offered these strategies as a means of helping children learn to manage worry, fear, and anxiety, they are equally effective in helping children learn to minimize and deal effectively with anger.

Anger causes a physical reaction in our bodies. Imagine how you might feel if you narrowly avoided an automobile accident due to another driver's negligence. Your heart might pound. You might find yourself gripping the steering wheel tightly. Your breathing might become quick and shallow. These reactions are a normal physiological response to stress, fear, and anger.

When we become angry, our bodies go through a preprogrammed routine. We suggest "preprogrammed" because every human being, regardless of age, race, culture, or ethnicity, experiences the same reaction to varying degrees. This reaction affects the entire body. The heart beats faster. The face flushes. Even hearing is affected as our ears tune out the range of the human voice! Little surprise, then, that many parents report that when their children are angry they "seem not to hear what is being said to them."

Potentially, guided imagery, progressive muscle relaxation and deep breathing can be used by teens. However, by adolescence, your child is not going to be as receptive to these tools if the information comes from you, the parent. A trusted friend of the family or a favorite relative may be a better source. Of course, if you provide a positive model for the use of these tools, it increases the chances that your child will make use of them. If it is apparent that when angry you will take a break and use one or all of these techniques to enable you to approach the situation with calm, your teenager benefits and can better appreciate his potential.

Relaxed Breathing
One of the quickest ways to send the body a physical message to calm down is to breathe slowly (without holding your breath). Model this type of breathing for your child and encourage him to follow your lead and breathe at your pace. For children eight years old or younger, one second in and one second out is a good place to start. For children ages nine and older, two seconds in and two seconds out is suggested. These breathing rates are suggestions, but individual comfort levels with inhalation and exhalation will vary from child to child. With more practice, your child will likely be able to comfortably extend inhalation/exhalation times.

When doing deep breathing, teach your child to breathe from the diaphragm rather than from higher up in the lungs (called *shallow breathing*). The stomach should move up and down while breathing, not the chest.

Again, this sends a physical message to the body to relax and calm down. Shallow breathing could send the opposite signal and trigger the "fight or flight" response. At the very least, it is a much less efficient way to get the body to calm down.

For the optimal benefit of the deep, paced breathing, encourage your child to breathe in through his nose and out through his mouth. Breathing in through the nose moistens and warms the air going to your child's lungs, thereby preventing a dry throat or other discomfort. This, too, sometimes takes some practice.

Teaching relaxed breathing to your child. When initially teaching this technique to your child, it is helpful to identify how she breathes. Have your child place one hand on her chest and one hand on her stomach. As she breathes normally, the hand on her stomach should rise on inhalation more than the hand on her chest. If the chest moves more, your child is more of a chest (or shallow) breather. It is often helpful to model this yourself. Adults are usually good examples of "chest breathers"! As we get older and deal with the daily stresses of life, it is not uncommon for many of us to gradually develop a shallower breathing pattern. However, if you've ever watched a sleeping baby, you'll notice her stomach rises significantly higher on inhalation than her chest—this is how we were born to breathe!

For younger children (ages four to eight), the image of the tummy as a balloon (let your child pick the color) can be helpful. Have your child imagine the balloon filling up when inhaling, and letting all the air out while exhaling. If your child is unsettled by imagining a balloon in her tummy, let her imagine that the belly button is rising up and then sinking back in. It may take some creativity on your and your child's part, but try to find an analogy or theme that your child can imagine and understand, and stick with it.

For older children, deep breathing can be easily explained and modeled by placing a hand on the stomach and chest, encouraging the child to raise the stomach more than the chest. Describing the fight-or-flight system of the body is also helpful for older children and adolescents. Explaining that fear, worry, and anxiety or panic are physiological responses may provide a greater sense of control than children thinking "It's all in my head."

Troubleshooting relaxed breathing problems. It will take your child some time and practice to learn relaxed breathing. If he seems to be having trouble in a particular area, consult the following tips for help.

- *Feeling lightheaded when attempting deep breathing.* Your child may be inhaling too deeply and/or holding his breath. Encourage and demonstrate relaxed, paced breathing. Correct deep breathing doesn't require a huge intake of air and should sound just slightly louder than normal breathing. If your child seems to be holding his breath to mimic the breathing pace you've modeled, let him experiment and set a more comfort able pace.

- *Stomach rises on exhalation rather than inhalation.* If this occurs, your child is using her stomach muscles to push out her tummy. The natural expansion of the diaphragm should occur on *inhalation.* Coach your child on the correct breathing technique. If possible, allow her to watch and listen to a baby sleeping—babies are excellent models for the correct breathing technique.

Progressive Relaxation

Along with practicing relaxed breathing, you and your child can learn to relax your muscles to achieve overall relaxation *(progressive relaxation).* The goal is to relax individual muscles or muscle groups one at a time rather than trying to "force" the entire body to relax all at once. Like deep breathing, progressive relaxation takes time, practice, and concentration. Just as with learning to ride a bike, at first it takes a concerted effort to learn proper technique. With each practice session, however, the body will become more and more efficient in reaching a state of relaxation.

Children can learn to take themselves through the relaxation technique, but initially parents should guide the relaxation efforts. As the child becomes more proficient, he may also enjoy making a tape of either his voice or his parent's voice, talking through the various muscle groups. Suggested muscle groups include the following:

- Facial muscles (forehead, cheeks, jaw)
- Neck and shoulders
- Upper arms
- Lower arms
- Hands and fingers

- Back and stomach
- Upper legs
- Lower legs
- Feet and toes

Although personal preference may dictate the order of the progressive relaxation, you might find it helpful when first starting out to begin with the facial muscles and gradually move down to the toes.

When first learning progressive relaxation, it can be difficult to determine how relaxed the muscles are. The tension/relaxation method helps you feel the difference between tense muscles and relaxed muscles, and therefore may help children learn to relax their muscles more easily. Focus on a specific muscle or muscle group, contracting the muscles for one to three seconds and then releasing the contraction.

Teaching progressive relaxation to your child. Children under ten years of age may best understand a state of relaxation as being like a floppy doll or puppet. Modeling tension (using the analogy of a scarecrow or robot) and relaxation can be an excellent way to teach younger children. For children ages ten and older, describe relaxation as becoming soft as a pillow or cloud, or "melting" into the cushions of a couch or bed. Encourage your child to come up with her own analogy or method of relaxing. It is important to take into account her fears or worries when facilitating relaxation. For example, a child with a fear of heights probably would not relax trying to become "soft as a cloud."

If your child struggles to get relaxed, have him notice how his body feels when he *first* wakes up, before stretching or moving in the bed. Have him notice body position, how it feels in the bed, whether his limbs feel heavy, and so on. This often helps give children an idea of how their bodies feel when they're relaxed.

Troubleshooting progressive relaxation problems. If your child has difficulty with progressive relaxation, consult the following list for help.

- *Laughing when attempting relaxation.* Laughing is great medicine and should be encouraged in appropriate circumstances. However, if it continuously interferes with attempts at relaxation, state matter-of-factly (not punitively) that you'll help your child try to relax later when she's more focused. Then try an hour or so later.
- *Can't seem to focus.* Try relaxation later in the evening (but not right before bedtime) when your child has started to wind down.
- *Has trouble relaxing body parts.* Encourage your child to try to relax his whole body at once (rather than progressively).
- *Can't find the "right time" to practice.* Try relaxation after a low-key activity, such as a bath, rather than after a high-stimulus activity, like playing video games.
- *Complaining of not being able to relax.* Review the techniques your child is using and ask yourself the following questions:
  - Is the analogy inappropriate or uncomfortable for my child? (For example, a young boy may not want to be "like a doll.") If so, try another.
  - Is the environment distracting? Is the family dog barking? Is the television too loud? Are siblings making noise or interrupting? If so, find a quiet spot.
  - Is the time of day inappropriate? (For example, your child is inside trying to practice relaxation when all the neighborhood kids are outside playing.) If so, change the time.
  - Are *you* a source of stress? Does your child appear to feel anxious having to "perform" in front of you? Does your child respond to your coaching or direction with resistance or passivity? If so, try lowering the bar by providing an easier goal and more empathy.

Guided Imagery

Guided imagery is often used in conjunction with breathing and relaxation techniques to reduce feelings of fear, worry, or anxiety. Have you ever imagined yourself in a quiet, safe, soothing place when you were under a great deal of stress? You probably noticed that doing so created a physical relaxation response in your body. Imagery generates positive thoughts and images that displace negative ones, a mental distraction that may help derail the runaway train of uncomfortable thoughts and feelings.

Like relaxation, guided imagery begins with a detailed step-by-step procedure to help children imagine a certain scene or place. Countless themes are possible, but common images include being on a soft cloud, lying under a rainbow, sitting on a beach, or lying on a blanket in a meadow. The images may be real places or make-believe places. Remember to use an image or theme that is relaxing and does not provoke anxiety. For example, children with allergies or asthma probably wouldn't become more relaxed imagining themselves in a meadow. (Imagining cold places, such as a ski resort or on top of a snowy mountain, is not recommended because it can increase body tension.) Encourage your child to discover her own preferences.

As with the other techniques we've discussed so far, learning guided imagery will initially take some time and effort. With guidance and practice your child can master this beneficial and enjoyable technique.

Following are two examples of guided imagery "scripts" that can be used or modified to create the most effective scene for your child. A helpful technique for some children is to read, or have the parents read, the scripts into a tape recorder. The recording can then be used to guide the child as he listens to a description of his ideal relaxing place.

Sample 1 (may be modified to suit your child's age)

Now I am going to sit back, relax, and close my eyes. Today I am going to go to a special place where I am as free and relaxed as possible. This place is secure and safe. My special place is a haven, a place where no one else has ever been. I want to go there now.

I am in a forest of Aspen trees. I see the beauty of the white bark against the bright autumn-changing leaves. The weather is cool but not cold, and there is a slight breeze. The breeze rushes through the tops of the Aspens, causing some leaves to fall, the others making a wispy melody. I can hear this sound, and it relaxes me.

It is a beautiful afternoon; the sun is shining brightly and the sky is a deep blue. The sun falls through the Aspens and forms a circle of sunlight on the plush green ground. I lay down in this circle. I am on a soft blanket. My hand brushes over it and I feel the softness on my palms and fingers. As I lay down I feel the sunlight on my face and hands. I feel bathed in peace and have a deep sense of comfort.

I take a deep breath as I let the peace and softness of this place spread through my entire body. I hear the sounds of the leaves and the flowing of the clear, cool water of a nearby brook as it tumbles over the shiny, glistening rocks. With each breath I become more deeply relaxed, every muscle in my body becoming heavy, warm, and relaxed. I become more calm and secure with the peaceful and hypnotic sounds of the leaves, whispering to me that I am safe and protected.

Sample 2

Now that I am relaxed and my body is free of muscle tension, I want to imagine my special place. It is a beautiful, warm day. The sun is shining brightly and there is a cool breeze. I am standing in a meadow of colorful wildflowers. Before me is a beautiful scene of nature. As I reach my place, safe around the beautiful flowers, I sit down.

I am proud and in awe of my view of the meadows and streams. I lean back against the single tree in the meadow—a large oak with protective limbs. The sun is able to make its way through the leaves, and it falls on my face and shoulders. I feel this warmth throughout my body. I am totally at peace. I feel the warmth of the sun as it radiates across my body and onto my shoulders. I feel the slight breeze in my hair while I hear the rustling of the leaves in the trees. My special place is calm and quiet. I am completely relaxed, taking in every sound and sight of the beautiful surroundings. My body feels no tension or stress, only relaxation. I feel the strength of the sun on my shoulders. My body takes in every soothing beam of warmth, further increasing the relaxation in my shoulders. I am completely at peace, and I am safe here in my special place.

Teaching guided imagery to your child. Describing imagery and its benefits to children can be difficult. In a sense, we are attempting to "trick" our body into thinking it is somewhere else—somewhere that is calm and relaxing—using only our minds. You or your child might be skeptical, wondering, "Can the way I think *really* change how my body is feeling?"

The answer is *absolutely!* Think of how you feel when you're angry—your stomach might hurt, you get a headache, you feel sweaty or jittery—these are body sensations that are caused by our *thoughts.* In that sense, using guided imagery is like fighting fire with fire.

An excellent demonstration to show how our thoughts and images can affect our body is the pickle trick. (If your child dislikes pickles, think of a favorite food you can use in this exercise.) Have your child close her eyes and imagine herself on her bed (or the family couch, or another place she likes to lie down). Gradually and slowly talk her through the following phases, providing enough detail to help her imagine the scenes but not so much that she loses interest: getting up from the bed, walking down the hall to the kitchen, describing the kitchen, walking toward the refrigerator and opening it to see a big jar of pickles, taking the pickles out of the refrigerator and placing them on the counter, opening the jar and taking out the biggest pickle, lifting it up to her mouth, and taking a big bite. This will probably help your child experience the sensation of biting into a pickle, even though she only imagined it.

Troubleshooting guided imagery problems. When children complain that they can't imagine, try a few of the following exercises. These techniques can often help children become more confident in their ability to use imagery as a relaxation tool.

- Encourage your child to imagine, or see in his mind, his dog, a friend, or a teacher. Then ask questions: for example, "When you are thinking of your dog, what is he doing? Is he sitting, standing, or lying down?"
- Have your child imagine and describe a scene in her mind, such as a favorite playground or a landmark or event from vacation last summer.
- Have your child imagine the route from home to a favorite restaurant, school, or friend's house, describing all of the landmarks, traffic lights, and other highlights along the way.

Self-Talk Strategies

The words we use to describe our experiences to ourselves and others are powerful in shifting angry thoughts and feelings. For example, one person can perceive another as slow while a second perceives the same person as careful. Mental health professionals sometimes refer to the words we choose to describe ourselves and others as *semantics*. Semantics reflects the meaning of language—in this case, the personal meaning we assign to the behavior of others, as well as our thoughts and feelings. *Self-talk strategies,* changes thinking, and helps children use language to redirect and guide their behavior.

In this section we will describe three semantic strategies to reduce angry feelings. *Self-talk* is the chatter in our heads, the things we tell ourselves, the internal dialogue we have throughout our waking hours. The *positive self-talk* technique consists of making statements to affirm feelings of control and to combat negative self-talk that exacerbates or perpetuates angry feelings. *Mental distraction* involves engaging in a mental task or exercise to compete against intrusive negative thoughts. *Debriefing* is simply talking about and analyzing our emotions and frustrations with a caring, supportive person.

Positive Self-Talk

The scripts for positive self-talk can be specific ("I *will* get back in control") or general ("I am safe; I am OK"). The method of self-talk also varies; some children prefer to repeat one phrase over and over, whereas others may wish to engage in a "running commentary" about their thoughts, feelings, or the environment around them.

One popular self-talk technique is the *stop-think* method, in which you teach your child to identify the initial feelings or thoughts of worry, fear, and anxiety and then say or think "Stop!" At that point, encourage the child to think of an affirming, relaxing, or realistic (rather than irrational) thought. You can help identify thoughts that are comforting and useful for your child. If he has a specific fear or worry, realistic and factual information can provide a wealth of fear-fighting thoughts. It is important for parents to discuss reality and facts with their children, rather than saying "Oh, it's not real—don't worry about it." Explain *why* something is not real (for example, a movie villain) in a matter-of-fact fashion. However, don't expect that the child will automatically believe you or suddenly not be frightened anymore. It is OK for children to be skeptical when someone tells them the basis for their fear is not real. The goal of self-talk is to provide children the information and courage to gradually convince themselves.

Here are some examples of affirming thoughts:
- I am OK.
- I am safe.
- I am strong.
- I am not afraid.
- I have practiced and am prepared.
- I will try my best on the test tomorrow.

Relaxing or pleasant thoughts might include the following:
- I am in such a warm and comfortable bed.
- I can't wait to see Grandpa this weekend!
- I will get to make cookies when I get home.
- I get to spend the night at my friend's house.

Realistic thoughts such as the following can calm fears:
- Ghosts aren't real.
- That bad guy in the movie is just an actor.
- Mom and Dad locked all the windows and doors.

Mental Distraction

Mental distraction consists of thinking of a task that distracts the child and interrupts the negative thoughts that perpetuate or exacerbate anger. As with self-talk, mental distraction works best when children or teens employ it at the first sign of anger. The themes for mental distraction can be endless, but some common techniques include the following.

Serial 7. Have the child think of a number and then subtract 7 from that number, then 7 from that number, and so on. Encourage older children to start in the hundreds; younger children can start around 50 and use their fingers if needed. This is a fun distraction for kids who like math, but it might provoke more anxiety in those who don't.

How-To. Have the child or teen mentally talk through (or even mentally envision through imagery) how to do something—how to build a Lego fort, how to fix a skateboard, how to make pancakes, and so on.

Lists. Have the child think of lists for something: the ultimate trip to a candy store, what she wants to take on vacation, what she wants to do with Grandma or Grandpa, and so on.

Debriefing

Most of us at one time or another have been greatly relieved by "talking out" problems, worries, or uncomfortable situations. Friends or family members who are ready to lend an ear and provide comfort, suggestions, and reassurance can help tremendously when we are distressed. In a sense, this is what *debriefing* is. Debriefing includes identifying, questioning, discussing, and generating strategies and solutions to address the causes of anger. For children, debriefing can help slow down the "runaway train" that often causes feelings of uneasiness and distress. For teens it is part of their social interaction and can help them gain perspective. As most parents know, telling children "It's OK—don't be angry" or, for that matter, "Try harder," does not usually stop increasing feelings of anger.

Children who have the opportunity to discuss the things that bother them and are given accurate (and realistic) facts have the information and power they need to learn to confront negative thoughts and feelings. The parents' role in debriefing is to help children and teens identify, through guided questioning, the whats, whys, and hows that are causing distress. By engaging in this process of "thinking out loud" children can often gain insight about how to address and cope with their worries.

The following types of questions are samples of what can be used to begin the debriefing process.

1. What happened that made you feel angry?
2. When did you start feeling angry about that?
3. What was different that made you feel angry this time?
4. What was your first thought about that problem?
5. How did your body feel?
6. What makes you feel safe or strong?

Once children have started to discuss the whats, whys, and hows, parents can provide specific information and reassurance that can be the basis for self-talk techniques. It should be emphasized that the process of debriefing is not to convince children that there is no basis for anger. With teens it is doubly important not to be judgemental. While parents can view debriefing as a fact-finding and fact-giving mission, it is important to provide empathy and not be dismissive of their child's distressed thoughts and feelings.

Practice Effective Communication

Effective communication is a critical process in helping children manage anger. To communicate effectively, parents must listen and learn. For a variety of reasons, even well-intentioned parents communicate in ways that at best possess little chance of nurturing resilience and at worst actually chip away at a child's resilient mindset. The challenge of simultaneously keeping our goals in mind and communicating effectively, free of the emotion that often accompanies problems with our children, is daunting. When parents are frustrated, they sometimes bring their own excess baggage from the past into the present situation.

To practice effective communication, ask yourself the following questions:

- Do my messages convey and teach respect?
- Am I fostering realistic expectations in my children?
- Am I truly listening to and validating what my children are saying?
- Do my children know I value their input?
- Am I helping my children to appreciate that mistakes are part of the process of learning?
- Am I comfortable acknowledging my own mistakes and apologizing for them?

Three key obstacles can prevent even well-meaning parents from communicating effectively with children and teaching children effective communication skills:

- *We practice what we have lived.* Our personal history—our experiences, both good and bad—shapes our behavior. If a parent grew up in a home in which the family communication style did not provide opportunities to learn to manage anger, it is typically more difficult (but certainly not impossible) for that parent to communicate in ways that help children develop anger management skills.
- *Anger clouds effective communication.* As we have discussed, it is difficult to communicate effectively when angry.
- *We sometimes believe that our children's goal is to wear us down.* All children test their parents at times. When limits are set, children may not respond with thank-yous. However, if limits and goals are established in an atmosphere free of anger and tension, children will feel safe and secure. If parents, however, view children's anger and questioning of their authority as evidence that

they hold a personal vendetta against them, their communication will reflect and reinforce this negative perception and breed further power struggles.

To communicate effectively with your children, we suggest following some simple guidelines.

Be Proactive
Take advantage of spontaneous moments for communication. Also, schedule specific family times to discuss important issues. But remember that communication should not be confined to a scheduled, once-a-week event. Parents should communicate with their children every day. Being proactive means accepting the responsibility of communicating with children about important subjects before they become problems.

Become an Active Listener
Too often, when parents think of effective communication they think of how they might best express themselves. While expressive language is a major component of communication, parents must begin by making certain that they listen and learn before they seek to influence. To be an active listener implies that parents begin without assumptions. Parents who are active listeners truly attempt to understand the verbal and nonverbal messages conveyed by their children. They perceive the feelings, thoughts, and beliefs they are communicating, and they do not let their own agendas or need to get their point across interfere with their ability to appreciate what their children are attempting to communicate.

Validate and Affirm
It isn't enough to listen. You must validate what your children are saying and confirm that they have been heard. Effective communication will be derailed if you fail to validate what your children are telling you. Validation helps children believe that adults listen to and respect their views. This creates a climate in which anger is less likely to occur and communication can be more effective.

Use Nonjudgmental and Nonaccusatory Communication
This requires empathy and validation. When upset with children, it is easy

to adopt an accusatory mode and to make assumptions about their behavior that only fuel further anger, criticism, and judgment. If we want children to learn from us rather than resent us, we must minimize accusatory messages.

Communicate Clearly and Succinctly
Parents often attempt to communicate so much information at one time that their child simply can't take it all in. Routine communications with our children should be brief and focused. Communication is a lifelong process. Not everything must be accomplished in one discussion. If too much information is offered at once, particularly as children are agitated or angry, they may become overwhelmed, incapable of processing anything they are told. Teens, in particular, hear long discussions as sermons and may shut down. In such situations, say to your child, "Everyone is getting so angry, but nothing is being accomplished. This is not the best time to continue this discussion. We all need a break."

Model Honesty and Dignity
Parents sometimes are not forthright with their children, and too often they err on the side of fostering a cloak of secrecy in the household. We are not suggesting that parents discuss issues that are highly personal or beyond children's emotional or cognitive capabilities. We are suggesting that children typically cope more effectively when informed about distressful news and what the parents are doing to address the situation. A child's fantasy about the secrets in the house may intensify rather than lessen anxiety and anger.

Accept Repetition
Children may have to hear a message many times before they understand and incorporate it into their thinking. While this may seem obvious, many parents become annoyed if children ask the same questions multiple times. Separate a child's need to change your mind from his need to know and understand. Parents must be prepared to answer the same question from children repeatedly. Sometimes questions represent children's attempts to understand their world, develop and feel a sense of mastery, gain knowledge, and solve problems.

Make Humor an Integral Part of Your Communication

Playfulness and humor are important ingredients in the communication process. Humor has repeatedly been found to help children cope with adversity. Be careful, however, to consider how it will be received by others. If you are angry with your children and they are angry with you, jocularity can easily be experienced as sarcasm. Humor should be used to create a warm environment in which parents and children feel comfortable and in which children will more readily learn.

Summary

There are acceptable and unacceptable ways of dealing with anger. This step reviewed a number of effective strategies to help you help your children reduce angry outbursts in the face of frustration, express anger appropriately, and maintain focus on effectively resolving problems. By incorporating a variety of anger management strategies into your daily interactions with your children, you provide the instruction and modeling they need to develop these skills. Some children may develop these skills easily, while others may require repeated guidance and instruction. You may need to enlist the aid of others to reinforce the concept. As with teaching children other skills, such as swimming or riding a bicycle, your mindset must be to provide your child sufficient opportunities in a patient, supportive atmosphere to develop essential anger management skills. Just as some children with poor coordination require many more opportunities and directed instruction to learn to ride a bicycle, so too will some children require much more time to develop the skills to effectively manage anger. With patience and support, all children can learn to effectively manage and work through anger.

Step 5

Develop a Daily Management Plan and Put It into Action

Despite the fact that some children are born more irritable and quick to anger, parents may feel as if a child's ability to handle frustration and disappointment is a measure of their ability to parent. When outbursts occur despite parents' best efforts, there is a real sense of frustration.

Hearing yourself barking directions and issuing ultimatums while knowing that your child is not going to do what you want anyway is emotionally draining. Often there's a palpable tension in your household—a feeling that an explosion is waiting to happen. At times you're overwhelmed by a sense of helplessness. At other times you're resolved to "get a handle on" the situation or behavior, but your inability to do so makes you feel worse, which, in turn, adds to the anger.

Your unpredictable child is living in an unpredictable household. Emotional volatility—frustration, depression, and anger—accompanies effort upon fruitless effort to "fix" the situation. Family functioning seems at the mercy of this child. Even if that isn't actually so, it certainly feels like it. If the child's behavior is negative and unpredictable, then the household is, by definition, in chaos. The result is an angry household.

What can be done to influence that three-step process of anger—the internal emotion, the external behavior, the response from the environment—even before the emotion? Too often the focus is on conflict resolution instead of prevention. Parents can take steps with the more reactive, volatile child that will decrease the chances that there will be such intense emotion.

Planned Parenting

A big step toward reducing the number of situations that produce anger is to practice *planned parenting* rather than reactive parenting. It isn't easy at first. It entails discussing priorities, specific behaviors, approaches, and responses *before* situations develop. It requires thinking about who your child is (instead of who she is not). It means determining which situations are most stressful and which behaviors you want to change, then providing the structure to make it happen. This is quite different from reacting to situations as they occur (usually over and over).

Many explosive situations are varying expressions of the same root causes arising day after day. These situations repeatedly result in the same frustrations: tempers flare and meltdowns occur. Parental frustration fuels child anger, which, in turn, fuels parental anger. Avoiding conditions that result in meltdowns is a key component to planned parenting.

If trips to the grocery store end in argument and punishment, don't take your child to the store—or go with a short list so you're not there long. Prepare the child by having a list with one empty line that is his to fill with one item he would like to purchase. The one line is a visual message that he can pick only one item, not one from each aisle.

If a child's fatigue when she returns from an overnight stay with a friend makes it difficult for her to participate in family activities the next day, don't plan activities the day after an overnight. Better to reschedule or to do the activity without the child than to have another angry meltdown.

Know your child as he *is,* not who he ought to be or who you thought he was. Thinking that he ought to be able to do something or that he already can do it will inevitably lead to frustration and failure. His age may not be a good indicator of his abilities: for example, maybe he *ought* to be able to make it through three brief stops, and maybe his younger brother can, but he can't. The fact that by fifteen he ought to be able to keep his room organized doesn't mean he can. And your thinking he *should* be able to doesn't make him able to.

Before you can make changes, you must see your child for who she is rather than who she is not, and value and build on her strengths. A realistic view of your child's strengths and "improvables" decreases the likelihood that inflated expectations will result in frustration for both of you.

Don't take bad behavior personally. The way we interpret our child's behavior plays a significant role in how we respond to that behavior. Take care not to attribute negative motives to your child's behavior; the moment you do, you will be more reactive than responsive.

Provide Structure and Predictability

Few things give a child a greater chance for success than living in a home with parents who can anticipate his needs and provide sufficient structure in his life until he acquires the skills to do so for himself.

All children need structure in their lives. Some can develop it for themselves, but most need adults to provide that structure for them. And some children need more structure than others do. In the same way, most kids prefer predictability. They like to know roughly how the day will go, what will happen if they misbehave, and that there will be no school on holidays. For some children, however, predictability isn't merely desirable or preferable—it's essential. Without it, they feel out of control or overwhelmed by the moment. This can easily result in anger. When they feel out of control, they may act that way.

Establish Routines

One of the first steps in reducing household stress and putting a daily management plan into action is to establish routines that give children a sense of predictability. That means we have to determine what situations occur regularly and then establish a structure or sequence to be repeated each day. Planning routines based on the situations that occur most often is best for family functioning. Many times families focus on the most recent blow-up when trying to create rules or routines. But reactively addressing the exceptional situations (what to do when a relative comes to visit, for example), while important, is not as helpful as addressing the situations that occur often. If it happens every day, it is a good bet that establishing a routine related to that situation will help reduce anger and frustration in the household.

Routines mean repetition, and repetition means practice. Practice allows a child to become proficient (or at least better) at meeting the basic requirements by herself. This is helpful to all children, and essential for some.

Communication and concurrence between parents is a vital part of this process. Both must agree to look for and reinforce the same sequence of behaviors.

The process for establishing a routine or changing a specific behavior requires answering three questions:

1. What do I want the child to do instead of what he is doing?
2. How can I communicate this desired change to him in a visual format?
3. What will make compliance worth his while?

Many times, even everyday activities result in angry outbursts—on everyone's part. Even in the most frantic of households there are only three things that your child must perform daily, but may have trouble doing consistently: get up and get dressed, eat, and go to sleep. If only these three events went smoothly, you'd have a far calmer household.

Fortunately, you can devise routines to help your child accomplish these things. Most people establish routines by doing the same tasks regularly until the pattern becomes established. For children to establish patterns, they need a specific structure set up by someone else (you, perhaps with their input) that they can practice with reminders or prompts that do not entail Mom or Dad standing over and nagging or yelling at them.

Routines also keep adults honest so that we don't change our expectations. Let's be frank: on different days adults have different expectations for the exact same situation. This is reason enough for a lot of anger on both the child's and the adult's part.

The following guidelines will help you establish routines that are a vital part of your daily anger management plan. In addition, filling out this worksheet may assist you in this process.

Establishing Routines Worksheet

Whenever possible, include your child in the process of filling out this worksheet and establishing routines.

1. Identify anger-related situations that occur frequently.

2. Ask, "What do I want my child to do instead of what he's doing?"

3. Determine one to five things (depending on the child's age) that need to be accomplished as part of a routine.

4. Discuss and decide on the number of reminders needed.

5. Determine a time frame for completing steps.

6. Ask, "How can I put expectations and progress in a visual format?"

7. Develop documentation (chart, checklist).

8. Ask, "What would make compliance worth his while?"

9. Choose a reward for successful completion of the routine within specified time.

10. Review the steps of the routine, tools (checklists, timers), and rewards with the child.

Step 1: Narrow the Focus to What Needs to Be Done
To establish a routine you first must agree on what tasks are truly important—not your idealized vision of what your child ought to do. What *absolutely must* be included as a part of the daily routine? Decide which tasks are necessary and the sequence in which you want them to be done. If your child is over four, try to include him in this process. For teens this is essential. Children can better adhere to a routine they have helped develop. What does he think is important? How many reminders does he think he needs? Agree on a sequence and prioritize what's really important. This agreement becomes the standard so that everyone in the household knows what is expected and what to reinforce when the child gets it right.

For example, develop a list of items that might belong in his backpack each day. In preparation for the morning, have your child do some tasks the night before. Have him organize any equipment he needs the next day. This includes making sure his homework, field trip permission slips, and lunch money are in his backpack the night before and putting it by the front door. For at least two weeks initially, check the backpack items against the list the night before to ensure that the child has included all necessary items, then reinforce accordingly. The rule needs to be "If it's not in the backpack and down by the door, it doesn't go to school."

To help limit the morning checklist to what is really important, remember that the minimum standard is what the school accepts as "ready" when he walks in the door. They don't care if his bed is made. They *do* care if he's buck naked. The morning routine has to include getting up, washing, dressing, and eating breakfast by a certain time.

Step 2: Put It in Writing
When you give a direction and walk out of the room, your child has nothing to keep her on track. To her, you are a walking, talking prompt to follow your directions. But obviously, you can't be around all the time—nor should you be, because our ultimate goal is for her to become able to manage her own routines. Making a list can help her get to that point, reminding the child what she's expected to do. Place the list where your child will see it every time she needs to use it, or give her a new copy to use every day.

Step 3: Reinforce Routines with Incentives for Performance
Now the challenge is to find something to associate with it that is so important to the child that she will use the list on a daily basis. What works

as a reward may change and needs to be reviewed on a regular basis.

Determining what is an effective reinforcer is key. Many techniques, including praise and privileges, can act as meaningful rewards. Some effective rewards for younger children might include the following:

- Television privileges (specified time limit)
- Computer games (specified time limit)
- Video games (specified time limit)
- Playing outside
- Soda or ice cream
- Playing at the park
- Video arcade
- Ordering pizza in
- Chore pass (earning a pass out of a regular chore)
- Allowance or money
- Fast food meal
- Small toy or selection from privilege grab bag
- Extension on lights out (15 to 30 minutes)
- Spending the night at a friend's house or letting a friend spend the night
- Dressing up in adult clothes
- A "date" with a parent
- Having a friend over for dinner
- Camping out in the backyard
- Planting a garden
- Choosing the radio station in the car

For adolescents, any of the rewards just listed might work, in addition to the following:

- Phone in bedroom (limited phone privileges)
- Time to talk on phone
- Screen time (time to use any screen—TV, video game, computer)
- Curfew extension
- Learner's permit or driver's license
- Behind-the-wheel practice
- Use of car (specified purpose and time limit)
- Use of Internet
- CDs or DVDs

Whatever reward is chosen, it must be powerful enough to provoke the child to persist in trying to behave appropriately even though it is difficult.

What would make it worth it for the child to remember and do what is expected? Remember, most children don't want to misbehave. They are handling their world the best way they know how at the moment. The goal is simply to give the child a reason to get it right.

For easily distracted, oppositional, or younger children, prioritize the checklist even further by giving larger incentives for the more important items (such as getting up and dressed) and smaller rewards for any lower-priority items (such as making his bed or cleaning dishes). Make some things optional. Require your child to do everything on the basic list first and allow him to earn bonuses for completing optional items.

Consider one aspect of your daily life and determine whether you have taken the following steps.

1. Narrow the focus, making sure expectations are reasonable. Can your child do it without you, or does she need a predetermined number of reminders?
2. Put expectations in writing so the *list* becomes the measure of success, not you.
3. Provide incentives for completing the tasks successfully.
4. Back off to allow your child the opportunity to be successful.

When you establish reasonable routines, you are adapting household procedures, not creating a new set of rules to fix a broken or angry child. It sends a positive message to everyone in the family. Moreover, the consistency of expectations will reduce the level of reactivity and anger.

Tools to Help Establish Expectations and Routines

Visual cues, which can take the form of checklists, schedules, calendars, or timers, are essential to establishing routines. These tools depersonalize directions so your child is less likely to get emotional about the situation. Visual cues convey a guideline, a time limit, a system of organization, a sequence, or a behavioral expectation. They are mechanisms to remind a child or adolescent of what is expected *so you don't have to.*

Checklists and Schedules

A short written list of two to six items not only establishes the steps of a routine, but conveys expectations and criteria for performance as well. Limit lists for younger children to one to three items; three to six items for adolescents. Write the list on an erasable white board, post it on a bulletin board in the bedroom, or put it on a Post-it note that you stick on your child's door. Whatever you do, put the list where your child can't miss it. Remind her to check off each task as it is completed. Use picture cues for very young children. When your child says she's finished, you both survey the results as compared to the list. Acknowledge successful completion of each step. Call your child's attention to items still incomplete before she moves on to another activity. This way, the list defines "finished," not you.

A list can also lay out a schedule. An afternoon schedule might look like the following:

- Snack
- Homework
- TV/free time
- Dinner

If your child asks to watch TV, refer him to the schedule. That way, the list—not you—reminds him that the policy is homework before TV.

Schedules visually demonstrate sequence to a child, thus making her world more predictable. A child enters a situation with a preconceived notion about what the outcome will be, and some of the worst meltdowns occur when a child's concept of outcome does not match reality. Some children have particular difficulty making transitions. Knowing what will happen, as well as what will not happen, helps prevent those meltdowns.

Try not to take this personally, but your children are not interested in going to the cleaners. It isn't one of their priorities. A list of intended errands, which shows the child that the shoe store is only one of the stops, reduces fallout. Remember this formula:

Checklists + Schedules = Predictability = Fewer Meltdowns

Calendars

Another useful tool for establishing children's routines is calendars. They provide visual documentation of daily activities and can be used to resolve conflicts between children's and parents' expectations. When a child comes home and asks to do something special, let the calendar convey the decision. To make this system work you need to wean yourself from that parental cop-out "We'll see," which usually means "Probably not" to you and "Yes" to your child. If it's no, say so; if you're not sure, set a definite time by which you will tell your child one way or the other. And if the answer is yes, mark the event on the calendar.

Timers

Timers provide visual and auditory cues to document time for your children. Children and adolescents think that they always have more than enough time to do things they don't like to do and not enough time to do things they enjoy, so when you stop a fun activity they want to shoot the messenger. A timer says "Time's up" so you don't have to.

Before your child turns on the television, sits down at the computer, or starts talking on the telephone, set a timer to determine when time for that activity has expired. Have the child set the timer, or at least ask "What happens when the timer rings?" to confirm that he understands the boundary. When it rings and he appeals or complains, your response can be: "I'd like you to have more time, but the timer rang." You can be on his side and still make clear that time is not something you control.

It is essential that you reinforce the timer's decision (even if your child strenuously objects). As long as you adhere to the policy that something happens every time the timer rings (and that "something" does not include resetting it) the timer will become the enforcer.

Timers are even more effective when paired with incentives. Reinforce compliance when the child completes the task before the timer rings. An incentive gives the timer special significance, giving him a reason to respond.

The timer can also be a tool that protects the child's interests in her struggle against you, the timekeeper. In the past, when she wanted your attention, often her request was met with that maddening response: "In a minute." But how long was that minute? A timer can hold us to the same standard we impose on our children. Try responding to your child's request for time and attention with this suggestion: "Get the timer and I'll set it for fifteen minutes. When the bell rings, I'll stop what I'm doing and come into your room." A child can better accept this answer. The result is less frustration and less anger. If you adhere to the timer whenever it is used, your child can trust it to get you to stop, as promised.

Of course, these visual prompts are only as successful as your support for their use. If you don't reinforce your child's use of the tools, they will be less effective.

Back to Mulberry Street

Remember the families on Mulberry Street? Some of them can reduce the frequency of angry outbursts with the use of these tools and some additional structure. For example, Ellen Reese needs short lists that detail steps of a task. As she completes each step and checks it off, there's a sense of accomplishment. Lots of positive feedback from her parents and teachers for the smaller accomplishments and a process that allows her to rate her own success will go a long way toward reducing her sense of inadequacy.

Similarly, Michelle Esken can benefit from the use of lists and visuals, in this case to assist what may be a processing issue. Because her parents attribute negative motives to Michelle's inability to meet expectations, she is hurt, frustrated, and angry. Michelle doesn't get it, and talking at her and punishing her won't help. Breaking things down into smaller steps and reinforcing incremental successes may not fix the learning issue, but it will increase her sense of accomplishment.

Richard Smith needs the predictability that routines can provide. With the move and his father's illness, nothing in his world is the same. Everything is changed—and changing. Sticking to basic, simple routines is very reassuring. Discussing the issues, allowing Richard the opportunity to ask questions, raise concerns, or maybe solve problems or vent, gives him information so that he has a better handle on what is happening. Parents need to remember that in the absence of information, children make up their own "facts," which are often based on their fears and therefore provoke anxiety.

Summary

If you can pare down expectations to what is truly essential, put them into a routine, document what you expect with a visual cue, and reinforce adherence to the routine, things will go more smoothly with your child who is struggling with anger.

Remember to talk up success. The more your child challenges you, the more difficult it is to stay positive. But all children benefit from praise, so make it a priority to give it often.

Providing structure and establishing routines is easier than you think. Although children have difficulty doing so on their own, you can help them if you remember to ask the following:

1. What do I want my child to do instead of what she's doing?

2. How can I put that in a visual format so she doesn't have to rely on me to tell her what to do?
3. What would make compliance worth her while?

Planned parenting may appear to be a daunting task as you begin to make changes. However, once a consistent routine is established, planned parenting is one of the most effective ways of reducing angry outbursts and establishing an atmosphere at home in which anger, when present, can be effectively managed. Doing so makes it easier to be positive in your approach to behavior change. If something works, figure out where else you can apply it.

When a problem occurs, reflect on what's worked in the past. Maybe all you have to do is adjust the routine. Move a chore or responsibility to another time of day when not as much is going on. Establish a procedure that allows for a change in chores every two weeks. Ask questions that are specific to that situation and make the necessary modifications.

Step 6

Assess and Solve Problems

There is little question that anger management is learned. Although neurobiology can have a significant influence on our ability to handle anger effectively, that ability is not really something we are born with. Many other factors influence our ability to manage anger, such as the behaviors our parents used to manage anger, or stressful situations or events in our lives. Even our past frustrations or experiences can affect how well we manage our emotions.

Proper perspective is essential to our ability as parents to model good anger management. If you get reports that your challenging child behaves like an angel at school, don't take this as some kind of personal insult. Instead, look at the upside. The child who goes out into the community and effectively handles daily demands and frustrations learned these skills at home. He didn't just acquire them by osmosis. The anger management skills he is demonstrating elsewhere are the ones he gained, at least in part, working through difficult situations at home. This is the child you raised.

As you begin to work with your child to assess and solve problems, it's important to avoid the tendency to affix blame. Remember that effective anger management is learned, and it may take your child a great deal of time to learn it. The child needs you to be patient and forgiving. And give your child the benefit of the doubt if you notice that he seems to manage his anger better outside the home or with others; try not to take personally what you perceive as different standards of behavior on his part.

Are You a Challenged Parent?

There is no better example of the proverbial emotional rollercoaster than raising a child. Feeling tired or overwhelmed one day can cause you to mismanage a conflict, and what you see as a challenge one day may not seem so bad the next. But even if you have fleeting moments where you feel successful, if the same conflict keeps happening day after day, despite your best efforts to change it, you are a challenged parent. You may fear that your child's difficult behavior is seen by others as a measure of your competency as a parent or person. Feeling this way can translate to reactive anger management and negative scripts.

Sometimes children seem challenging because you compare them with other children—with their siblings, other students in their class, or other children in the neighborhood. They may also be challenging because their temperament simply isn't a good match for your own. They aren't "bad" kids, nor are you a "bad" parent. You simply must learn different ways to deal with the challenges this child presents.

Likewise, the truly challenging child evokes a sense of desperation as parents attempt to better understand and manage her. This is any child whose behavior stymies parental attempts to change it, who holds the family hostage to her negative behavior. A challenging child is not just the child with the label; it is any child who has simply outstripped your ability to parent.

Sometimes you feel paralyzed by your child's behavior. You hear yourself reacting in the same way. You know it isn't going to work, but you don't know what else to do. So sometimes you do nothing. You let it go. You know that's not the answer, but you're afraid of making things worse. You may even "walk on eggshells" or stop going places as a family because you fear your child's disruptive behavior. If so, you're probably seething inside, furious with yourself and your child. Much of the time, you just react—with high-volume, over-the-top emotion. You go from *feeling* out of control to *having* no control. Sometimes it feels as if you resent your own child.

Don't be surprised at your reactions. Your emotions only prove you're normal. You obviously love your child. He's still living with you, isn't he? You haven't given him away yet (though the thought has probably crossed your mind more than once). But the frustration that results can escalate situations and cause anger.

Behavior Change Starts with You

Your child may lack the skills to express anger appropriately. As each maladaptive behavior has occurred, you've told him the behavior is unacceptable, compiling a list of things he cannot do when angry. But what have you told him about how he *can* express his emotions? You can be sure that sometime between birth and age eighteen, when your child will likely go to live someplace else, he will disagree with what you are saying. As parents you must communicate to your child ways he can appropriately say, "I disagree with you." These might include saying, "This stinks," but does not include saying "You stink." Or the child may ask for a reason for a direction in a calm tone or ask for clarification. If you aren't sure what is acceptable, how can your child know what he can do?

If your child knew the acceptable way to handle anger and it came easily to her, she would be doing it. Her inability to handle the current situation is, in part, escalating it. Yet each new incident is an opportunity to further the teaching process. What is she learning from you? Is the current situation an example of two people who lack good anger management skills? The emotion you show and the words you choose to express yourself are models of anger management.

As mentioned before, it is the parent's responsibility to set a good example. Although you may not be the cause of poor anger management skills, you are part of the solution. Change in your child's behavior starts with you.

Effective Punishment

The most challenging, angry children receive the most criticism and punishment. Unfortunately, this pattern may result in a child developing a tolerance for punishment. The child continues to repeat the behavior and parents ratchet up the level of punishment, thinking that if the penalty is strong enough they will finally get through to him. The cycle repeats itself, escalating parental frustration and anger without any positive changes in a child's behavior.

Punishment is a necessary part of raising children, especially the more challenging ones. Knowing how to punish and, more important, what can reasonably be expected from punishment, can reduce the level of anger that usually ensues in the process.

Have Realistic Expectations

Punishment does not change behavior, especially when it is the only approach used, because it does not teach your child a better, more appropriate way to behave. The most you can expect is that it interrupt the behavior for the moment. And, if you're really lucky, your child may make the connection between the penalty and his own behavior—but not if he attributes the penalty to your outburst.

Punish Without Anger

Unfortunately, your child usually connects your behavior with the punishment. The more talking you do when a child misbehaves, the less likely your message will get through. If you look angry, it's hard for your child to associate his own behavior with the punishment. He thinks that it's a direct result of the fact that *you* lost it.

Right after your child is punished for doing something wrong, her thoughts are focused on escaping an uncomfortable situation. So limit communication to a brief message that identifies the rule that was broken and the associated consequence, stated in a matter-of-fact tone: "The rule is 'In bed by 9:00.' It's 9:45. That will cost you 45 minutes tomorrow night. Tomorrow night you must be in bed at 8:15." No discussion, no accusations, no ranting and raving. This increases the likelihood that your child can separate what you say from how you say it. Trust that, no matter how well you state your views, your child isn't listening to your lecture.

The hardest thing for parents to do while delivering a punishment is to hold their own frustration or anger in check and curb their tongue. Emotion diminishes the capacity to think and speak rationally. And because this isn't one of those moments when your child is interested in hearing what you have to say, skip the lecture. The less said, the better. What you *do* say, say in an even tone. If your words are interpreted as threatening and angry, the response is likely to be some form of reactive lashing out. This only perpetuates a pattern of poor anger management.

Warn First, Then Punish

Children need to know ahead of time exactly what the consequences will be if they misbehave. When she says, "That's not fair," what she really means is, "I didn't know that was coming." If your child knows what will happen before the behavior occurs, she can make an informed decision about how she wants to behave.

If you're like most parents, right now you're probably thinking, "I've told him a hundred times. . . ." The problem is that your child could not be sure whether you'd snap on 78 or on 103. Which time would be a warning and which would result in enforcement? If you find yourself even thinking, "That's it, I've had it!" you're about to deliver an unwarned punishment. When you find yourself saying that phrase, your next words ought to be, "The very next time you do or say that, it will cost you . . ." and detail the negative consequences of the behavior. Then follow through.

Have a Set Beginning and End to the Punishment

To be effective, a punishment must have a set beginning and end. Many times your child responds angrily to punishment because she doesn't know how long the process will last. When administering a negative consequence, make it clear when it will be over and under what circumstances the process will end. Gauge it by a timer or let it continue until a specific task or chore is complete.

Impose Consistent Penalties

Gradually increasing a punishment inadvertently tells your child that the first time the negative behavior occurred it was not as important. If the behavior is a problem, it is a problem every time it occurs. Don't slowly up the ante; give the same punishment every time the problem behavior occurs. This is not an exercise to see at what point the lesson is learned.

For punishment to be effective, a penalty must be imposed every time the misbehavior occurs. Your child has to know there will be a consequence—and exactly what that consequence will be—every time he behaves badly.

If your teenager violates curfew, each ten minutes she is late costs her ten minutes off curfew the next night. Twenty minutes late means she must return twenty minutes early the next night. Likewise, a child who gets up ten minutes late in the morning goes to bed ten minutes early that night. Getting up twenty minutes late costs him twenty minutes at bedtime. When established in advance, the exact consequence can be based on the severity of the infraction.

Make Penalties Enforceable in Varying Circumstances
Effective punishment must also be enforceable in varying circumstances. That means the babysitter can levy the penalty the same as Mom or Dad, and that it will be imposed whether the behavior occurs in the grocery store, while riding in the car, or when surrounded by ten friends at the child's birthday party. If time or circumstance makes it impossible to implement the punishment at the moment of infraction, hand over an I.O.U. that signals that the punishment will still be implemented at a later time. Your child must understand that a specific behavior earns the punishment whenever it occurs, regardless of where you are.

Pair Punishment with Reward
Finally, because punishment used as the only mechanism to change behavior is not likely to work, pair a positive approach with it. If you are like most parents, you know all too well that punishing a negative behavior over and over does not work. The more difficult the child, the more likely it is that he lives in a highly punitive world. He has endured every form of negative feedback, yet still hasn't changed his behavior.

This is your opportunity to interrupt that negative, unproductive cycle. You are more effective when you convey to your child: "If you do this behavior it will earn you this privilege, and if you don't it will earn you this punishment." Specify what behavior you want to see and reward it when she does it. Positive acknowledgment, paired with punishment, judiciously applied, is the most effective way to change behavior.

The key to real behavior change is identifying and noticing positive behavior. Take the time to notice when your child manages anger effectively. Jump all over it. This is one of the best ways to clarify your expectations for anger management and will be better received than the punishment following the outburst.

Rules for Effective Punishment

- Have realistic expectations.
- Use a matter-of-fact tone; don't punish with anger.
- Warn first.
- Have a set beginning and end.
- Impose consistent penalties.
- Administer the punishment immediately when the infraction occurs.
- Acknowledge and reward the child's appropriate behaviors.

Bear in mind that punishment, when delivered to perfection, will not be well received. Not making the connection to her own behavior, a child often blames you for the punishment. So expect a negative reaction. It is unrealistic to think it will have the desired result right away. The outpouring of reactions is emotions—that's all. It is venting or an attempt to dissuade you from your mission to attach consequences to her behavior. Evaluate any set of procedures by its results, not by what a child says. Focus on the behavior: if it changes for the better, then the reinforcements and punishments you've selected are effective, regardless of your child's complaints.

On the other hand, if the angry outbursts persist and the behavior doesn't change in two weeks, reevaluate your approach. Involve your child in the process. Ask him to name one or two behaviors or situations that need work. When you decide what the incentives and punishments will be, seek his input. However, make clear that his input is not binding.

Posting a list of behaviors and infractions with both incentives and consequences is a way to increase consistency and reduce arguments. These lists make outcomes predictable and act as the arbiter so you don't have to. Being able to reference a list decreases the likelihood that you will feel the need to lecture, because the list says it all. Moreover, a visual cue makes it easier for the child to make the connection between his behavior and the outcome. (See Step 5 for more on creating and using these visual cues.)

As noted earlier, increased punishment can lead to increased tolerance for punishment. An even worse potential consequence of ineffective punishment is diminished self-esteem. If a child hears the message that she is bad often enough, she will act accordingly. Never lose sight of the power of praise and positive notice of what's going right to break the cycle of negativity. Affirm your child's good behaviors and traits and reinforce them daily. Include those on the checklist in order to prompt and encourage you. It's a start to changing negative scripts and it can open your eyes to the way the day-to-day challenges have diminished over time.

Think Ahead: Clarify Expectations in Advance

Remember that your goal is *planned* and *responsive* parenting rather than *reactive* parenting. Parents typically argue, blame, agonize, and commiserate in reaction to difficult situations. But that process does not result in clear thinking, meaningful changes in parenting, or advance planning for the next time.

All children need limits. Consistently enforced, clearly stated guidelines give them a sense of security and predictability. If your child knows in advance what is expected and what the consequences are of meeting or not meeting those expectations, then the outcome is the child's choice.

Often, parents communicate rules to their children only after they break them, leading to a lot of frustration for both parent and child. To help you understand how unfair this feels to a child, consider the concept of a "mystery speed limit day." Imagine that every Thursday is mystery speed limit day. You get in your car and, although you are in a hurry and the usual speed limit is 55, just to be safe you drive at 45 miles per hour. Within two miles a policeman pulls you over, explains that today's speed limit is 35, and writes you a ticket.

How do you feel? Frustrated? Angry? Are you looking for a target for that anger? Welcome to your child's world. He often thinks that he knows the rules, but they seem to keep changing. Every time he turns around, there's some new thing he's done wrong, some new rule he's violated. Furthermore, he hears from you that he "should have known better."

It's easier for your child to remember rules he helped develop, and it's easier for him to stay focused on behaviors he thinks are important to work on. So ask him what he thinks he needs to work on. Get his input on both rules and behavioral goals. Fewer is better. If the child is part of the solution, he feels less like he is the brunt or cause of the problem.

Rules do not in and of themselves prevent negative behavior. Many parents, thinking that rules are the answer, have a rule to cover every situation. Too many rules, in an effort to control, frustrate the child and defeat the parent. Further, this kind of overcontrol can result in rebellion.

86

It is impossible to monitor and be consistent with so many rules to enforce. A child cannot remember what you said this morning. How will she remember all those rules? If you assign yourself the responsibility of praising your child every day for each rule she is following, you will quickly narrow your list. If the rule is important, it warrants praise. Rules are one area where the maxim "Less is more" applies.

Behavior Change Is Gradual

Unrealistic expectations are one of the biggest obstacles to change. They can distort your definition of progress—the kinds of changes you will see, how long they will last, or how quickly you expect them to take place. Parents often have unrealistic expectations for their children's behavior. Even though parents don't consistently follow up on directions, they expect their children to respond immediately when a direction is given. By age five, most children have learned that if a direction is important, the parent will repeat it, and if the direction is *very* important he will repeat it at high volume. The increased decibel level, unfortunately, adds to the anger and resentment of both parents and children.

If your child is disrespectful, it is unrealistic to expect that anything will result in his holding his tongue from this day forth. If the frequency of negative comments decreases from three to two a day, that's progress. The goal is not that your child will *never* talk back, or that your child will *always* respond respectfully. The terms *never* and *always* do not apply to behavior. Behavior does not occur in absolutes, and thinking that it will only increases frustration. Any parent who waits for perfection is missing many opportunities to savor and praise improvement. If you don't notice the small changes, you won't see progress—and progress is success.

Look for Trends
Measure progress by trends. Everyone has bad days and moments. Is the positive behavior occurring, on average, more frequently? Improvement doesn't occur at a steady pace. The more challenging the situation, the more you must measure progress in small increments.

Progress is measured in steps. It doesn't happen all at once and it doesn't happen overnight. You need to recognize it when you see it—in whatever forms it takes. If you want a negative behavior to decrease, then progress is that behavior occurring less often, for a shorter duration, or at a lower intensity.

If Michael Kennedy has fewer meltdowns, that is progress worth noting. If parental expectation is that he won't have any more outbursts, that is unrealistic and they will fail to notice the progress he has made. Moreover, if Michael's tantrums are measured only in terms of how often they occur, his parents might continue to overlook success. By shifting the focus to duration, they may realize that Michael's outbursts now last only half as long. The steps they have taken *have* produced change. If frequency is their only measure, they might give up on an effective approach.

Anticipate the Ups and Downs
Be prepared for frequent setbacks. When positive change occurs, and it will, rest assured that whatever is going right will not last. The best behavioral changes, like the worst, invariably pass. That's inherent in raising any child. If you anticipate the lapses, you'll be less frustrated when they happen. Realistic expectations of inevitable setbacks reduce anger in both the parent and the child.

When improvement occurs, some parents fail to recognize it; others start thinking it signals a "cure." When the inevitable regression happens, they are more disappointed than if no change at all had occurred. Their inflated expectations resulted in increased frustration despite the improvement. Therefore, it is essential to narrow your focus, define changes in terms of improvement (not perfection), anticipate the ups and downs, and reinforce any success.

Power Struggles
Power struggles can take place over anything. What distinguishes them from ordinary disputes is the extent to which each side becomes entrenched, determined not to yield. Often, both parties lose perspective. What is said is unproductive and can, in fact, be hurtful and counterproductive. Whichever side prevails, the outcome is not worth the destructive process. You must learn how to deal with power struggles when your kids are young, because when they become teenagers the anger resulting from battles of this magnitude puts great stress on a changing relationship.

Good anger management may be a factor that determines the frequency of the inevitable power struggles between parents and their children. In the book *From Chaos to Calm,* co-author and parenting consultant Sharon Weiss, details the steps to dealing with power struggles. Although every family faces this problem at one time or another, some experience it more than others. Those families need to take extra measures to avoid the blowouts, reduce their intensity, and resolve them when they occur.

Avoiding Power Struggles
The most effective approach to power struggles is to not have them. You can avoid many by following a few general principles.

- Ignore minor misbehavior. Pick your battles carefully. You can't work on everything at one time. Constant criticism breeds hostile and resentful children, and it doesn't improve their behavior.

- Don't badger. Tormenting and belittling your child in any way only increases anger and animosity. Say what you have to say without attacking her.

- Avoid nagging, lecturing, and arguing. They don't work. Your child isn't listening to your words of wisdom—much less your sermon. So stop. If your child tries to argue, state your position calmly and walk away. Act—don't yak! If you're not there, there is no one with whom he can argue.

- Get out of the moment. Try to see the situation in terms of the big picture. Ask yourself if this one point is worth the toll the argument may take on your relationship with your child. Will an intractable approach further her understanding of the point you are trying to make? Can whatever you have to say wait until later? Can you express yourself in a constructive, nonthreatening, rational way?

- Plan ahead. Another way to reduce the frequency of power struggles is to have a plan for early recognition and intervention. First, together with your child list on paper the situations or issues that trigger power struggles. Next, develop a structure for handling them. Under what circumstances does the 9:00 bedtime change? What is the policy for last-minute requests to have a friend spend the night? What, if any, are the circumstances under which you will advance allowance? Think about these situations and plan for them ahead of time—not when you and your child are in a heated argument. Once you have determined procedures, discuss them with your child (and the rest of the family). Let everyone know what the outcomes will be when these situations are resolved smoothly and when they're not.

- Create strategies to disagree. Agree on ways for you and your child to disagree. Discuss how she can express anger, frustration, or disappointment without automatically triggering a negative response from you. Your child is guaranteed to feel all these emotions at some point. Notice acceptable ways she already uses to express her feelings. Suggest methods for her to say, "I think this is a really bad idea," without your immediately becoming defensive. Remember, there is no chance of raising a child without her disagreeing with you. If you haven't figured out an acceptable way for her to do so, she will continue to step over "the (undefined) line" and you will always be telling her what she did wrong.

Handling a Power Struggle

No magic phrase will turn around a situation when you're engaged in a power struggle. No pearl of wisdom from you will change your child's mind. Emotions are already so high that even if you *did* know the right words, your child wouldn't hear them. Continuing to talk to her will not help your child see the light and concede. She feels that as long as you stay in the room, she still has a chance to get you to see her point of view. Clearly, neither of you is listening to the other. Bear in mind the words of Will Durant: "Nothing is often a good thing to do and always a good thing to say."

Remember three things about power struggles:

1. *No one wins a power struggle.* Even if you get your way or your child ends up with exactly what he wanted, there is no winner. The emotional fallout, the residual feelings, do not go away easily—if they go away at all. More often, they fester and reemerge unexpectedly at another time.

2. *If you think you may be engaged in a power struggle, you are.* You can feel it in your body. Your stomach may be tied in knots or your jaw might be clenched. Whatever it is, pay attention to it. It's telling you that you are headed for or already involved in something you want to avoid at all costs. The only way out is to do something different.

3. *Because there can be no winner, the only solution is to disengage.* Walk away. Get out.

Taking a Break: How to Get from Argument to Discussion

Taking a break is an effective tool for disengaging when emotion is driving the discussion and anger is pushing it toward argument. Establishing a process to disengage ahead of time lets everyone know what the procedure is and what to expect. Discussion is less volatile when there has been time to gain perspective.

Identify those signs your child shows when he's just beginning to get angry. When the situation is tense, watch for those signs that your child is on the brink of a meltdown and take a break. Calling for a break increases the likelihood that you'll keep yourself under control and substantially reduces the chance that you will have one of those knockdown, drag-out, no-holds-barred power struggles.

A break in different rooms gives both you and your child time to calm down. Never push a child to talk before she has time to calm down. The result will be more of the same angry behavior that brought you to the present impasse. The break also gives you a chance to reevaluate how important your position really is. Are you blowing things out of proportion? Is the point you are trying to make really so crucial? Should you rethink your position? Sometimes you need to find a way to back down. Other times, reevaluation allows you to reconfirm your position's importance, whether or not your child can see its merits.

A break also gives you the opportunity to think through exactly what outcome you want. What's realistic? Boiled down to basics, it may be that you simply want him to follow your direction. Or there may be a specific behavior you want him to stop. He doesn't have to be thrilled about it. If you expect compliance with no negative attitude, you expect too much. A break gives you time to ask yourself whether the argument is a result of your need to have him accept the outcome happily.

Guidelines for Taking a Break

- Anyone can call for a break.
- Have predetermined signals you'll use to communicate the need for a break, such as a hand signal or phrase.
- Decide ahead of time how long a break will last (for example, fifteen minutes).
- Determine the place and length of time for follow-up discussion (for example, at the kitchen table for no more than fifteen minutes).
- Set a timer and take notes when you resume discussion. Each party must listen without interruption.
- A raised voice or name-calling ends the discussion.
- Decide ahead of time what the policy is for decisions resulting from the discussion. For example, no decision or change will occur at that time; decisions affect only future situations; or you will consider the matter and make a decision later.

Make it clear that whether the discussion resumes (thus giving your child the opportunity to be heard) depends on her limiting argumentative behaviors and sticking to the plan. When you return, bring paper and pencil to record your child's concerns. It is the opportunity to be an active listener. Remember to validate and affirm, remaining nonjudgmental and nonaccusatory. Recording what your child has to say is a way to practice active listening and communicate that she has been heard, two of the steps to good communication mentioned in Step 4. Be prepared to listen and to praise improvement in your child's method of expressing her concerns. If she states her position in a different way, or her wording or tone is less contentious or argumentative, praise her before you respond. Improvement is progress, and progress is success.

Allow your child to talk uninterrupted as long as he limits himself to stating his concerns. Name-calling and disrespectful language ends the discussion. But be realistic. Expect some attitude and be prepared for that tone that makes your blood boil.

When explaining the process, make it clear which decisions, if any, will be made on the spot. Your policy may be that the current conversation affects future situations but won't change the one now under discussion. Or you may take the information you have recorded into consideration and return with possible alternatives in an hour. This makes it clear that nothing will happen this minute. Whatever the procedures, you need to review them more than once or participants will return to old habits.

The steps for effective problem solving provide a format for follow-up discussions. Each of these has a role in the discussion following a break:

- Define the problem and agree that it is a problem.
- Consider two or three possible solutions and a likely outcome of each.
- Develop a way to remind each other if someone forgets to follow through.
- Agree on what to do if it doesn't work.
- Keep in mind that your child is learning from you how to handle disputes. If you blow your stack at the first sign of disagreement, she's not likely to develop much skill at conflict resolution. At the end of any exchange, what message do you want to leave with her? Certainly not "win at any cost."

Most of the children and adolescents we find most challenging were born better at argument and debate than we can ever hope to be. Some truly seem to enjoy it. These future lawyers are prepared to keep up the argument at all costs. When you try to leave the room, they will dog your steps and follow you. Persisting in the argument only gives them practice at something at which they already excel.

Be sure to include contingencies for these behaviors when you develop procedures for handling power struggles. They need to know the downside of perpetuating unproductive arguments. Children who relish a fight often lose sight of the original point. Once the discussion escalates, all they care about is winning. If this describes your child, remember the adage "Never wrestle with a pig. You both get dirty, but the pig has fun." Keeping this in mind may help you adhere to a plan that relies on disengaging from the situation.

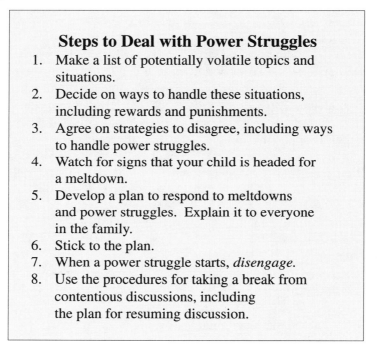

Steps to Deal with Power Struggles
1. Make a list of potentially volatile topics and situations.
2. Decide on ways to handle these situations, including rewards and punishments.
3. Agree on strategies to disagree, including ways to handle power struggles.
4. Watch for signs that your child is headed for a meltdown.
5. Develop a plan to respond to meltdowns and power struggles. Explain it to everyone in the family.
6. Stick to the plan.
7. When a power struggle starts, *disengage*.
8. Use the procedures for taking a break from contentious discussions, including the plan for resuming discussion.

Summary

Anger is an inevitable part of our lives. There are a number of things that can be done to reduce the chance that the outbursts associated with anger will be a daily challenge. When negative behavior, anger, and power struggles do occur, there are steps you can take to keep these situations from becoming the dominant theme in your family.

Don't overlook the benefit of added structure to help produce the desired change. An additional list or using a schedule, calendar, or timer can go a long way toward addressing the issue. Sit down with your child and establish procedures to discuss and resolve the really tough differences that become power struggles. Once any improvement occurs, jump on it. Notice it in a way that matters to your child.

Don't expect perfection, but be prepared to reward positive behavior. Children who are more oppositional need to experience both upsides and downsides of behavioral contingencies. So don't be discouraged if there are rocky periods. Expect to have to apply the negative consequences (which may only be that the child does not earn the privilege or other reinforcer). Anticipate ups and downs.

It is unrealistic to expect your child to get it right for the rest of his life. The purpose of punishment isn't to ensure that whatever behavior you're focusing on never happens again. Rather, your goal should be that the negative behavior doesn't happen as often, doesn't last as long, and isn't as intense.

The things you try may not get desired results right away. It's a learning process. You are learning new methods of conflict resolution and your child is learning—often from you—new ways to manage anger. It won't all happen overnight.

Finally, don't raise the bar too quickly. Once you have achieved some success, savor it. Don't increase your expectations just yet. Allow both you and your child the opportunity to enjoy the moment. Your child is not yet proficient at whatever has been achieved. It's still a work in progress.

Step 7

Instill a Resilient Mindset in Your Child

The dreams and wishes we have for our children include success in school, satisfaction in their lives, friendships, and the ability to become a functional member of their community. To realize these goals children must learn to cope effectively with their emotions, including anger. They must also possess the inner strength to deal successfully day after day with the challenges and demands they face. This ability to cope, feel competent, and overcome problems is called *resilience*.

Resilient children and adolescents are able to deal with stress and pressure. They bounce back from disappointments or adversity. They are capable of setting goals, solving problems, and acting responsibly. The skills that comprise a resilient mindset explain why some children overcome great obstacles while others become victims of the stresses and challenges they encounter.

Regardless of our ethical, cultural, religious, or scientific beliefs, developing a resilient mindset in our children is an essential parenting task. Children who have a resilient mindset carry with them a set of effective tools to deal with the problems they face in everyday life. Those prone to strong anger and other emotions fare better when they develop a resilient mindset. The concept of resilience includes a process of parenting that prepares children for success and happiness. Each interaction with our children provides an opportunity to help them weave a strong and resilient personal fabric.

Resilient children possess a view of the world that enables them to meet challenges and pressures and can translate this view into effective action. Resilient kids are hopeful and possess high self-worth. They feel special and appreciated. They have learned to set realistic goals and expectations for themselves. They are capable of solving problems and making good decisions. They view mistakes as challenges to confront rather than stresses to avoid. They have developed the interpersonal skills to deal successfully with peers and adults.

These qualities, however, are not acquired from a pill or a class. Rather, they are nurtured by parents who possess an understanding of important principles, ideas, and actions that contribute to the formation of a resilient mindset in their children. In Step 7 we provide strategies and guidelines to help your children develop five important resilience qualities. We introduce each quality and then offer several strategies and suggestions for you to consider in your day-in and day-out parenting. We believe that by using these strategies with angry children, parents strengthen their children's resolve and ability to benefit from interventions to develop anger management skills.

Feeling Special and Appreciated

When children feel loved and accepted they also feel special and appreciated. They believe they hold a special place in the hearts and minds of their parents. They sense that their parents truly enjoy being with them. In this way, parents can serve as *charismatic adults* in the lives of their children. The late psychologist Dr. Julius Segal introduced this term to describe adults who in their interactions with children convey love, acceptance, and support, qualities that help children feel unconditional love. Children gather unconditional love from such adults. This foundation is critically important for children because it not only lessens the frequency and intensity of anger, but when anger does appear it is expressed in more constructive ways. Feeling loved and appreciated is a cornerstone of a resilient mindset. It is little wonder that adults who have overcome great childhood adversity often attribute their success to at least one adult who was present for them during challenging times in their childhood and adolescent years.

Every interaction with your children is an opportunity to engage in a process of helping them feel loved and appreciated. Granted, in some situations, such as when we are frustrated and angry with our children, this is more difficult to accomplish. But those are the very situations in which it is vital to reinforce a resilient mindset. Here are six strategies to help you in this process.

1. Let Your Memories of Childhood Be Your Guide
Incorporate into your parenting practices those experiences that helped you
feel loved, as well as those that did not. Strive to avoid saying or doing
things that led you to feel less worthy, less loved, and more angry as a child
and, in many cases, as adults.

2. Create Traditions and Special Times
Creating traditions and setting aside special time with your children each
day, week, or month establishes an atmosphere in which they feel loved. In
doing so you convey the message to them that they are important to you
and you enjoy being with them.

3. Don't Miss Significant Occasions
If we are not present for the important events in our children's lives they
are likely to feel unimportant. Time spent with them, particularly during
special events, pays future dividends in the time they will invest in us as
adults, allowing us to share in their adult lives as well.

4. Be Demonstrative with Your Love
Although some parents find it difficult to display affection, we must all
strive to let our children know they are loved on a daily basis.

5. Build Up Your Children
As parents we routinely engage in a chipping-away process without realizing
it. We pronounce what our children are doing wrong rather than what they
are doing right. We correct rather than teach. In doing so, we erode, or fail
to reinforce, the features of a resilient mindset. It is difficult to develop a
sense of self-worth, security, and confidence in the presence of people who
are unappreciative.

6. Accept Your Children
A major challenge of parenting is accepting children for who they are and
not what we want them to be. The best way to help children change self-
defeating, angry behaviors is to create an atmosphere in which they feel

safe and secure. In such a climate they are able to recognize that what we are attempting to teach them is based firmly on our unconditional love. Unconditional love provides a powerful preventive antidote for angry outbursts.

Accepting Our Children for Who They Are

This last point deserves to be highlighted further. To nurture a resilient mindset requires that we love and accept our children unconditionally. Keep in mind that the concepts of fairness and acceptance are not synonymous with treating each child the same or having the same expectations and goals for each child. Fairness is demonstrated by responding to each child based on the child's particular temperament and needs. This type of acceptance is a foundation of resilience. Acceptance is rooted in unconditional love and provides an environment for the reinforcement of a resilient mindset. When children feel accepted they are more likely to be secure and confident, particularly in facing challenges and adversities.

A basic premise of this book is the acceptance by parents that some children temperamentally are born more likely to experience and be overwhelmed by anger. As children grow, differences in temperament are manifested in the ways they learn, the activities they choose, and their ease in dealing with daily life. We must avoid falling into the trap of telling our children we accept them, but . . . (that is, we accept them, but only if they behave or achieve in certain ways—this represents conditional love). Acceptance must serve as the link between our love and the process of defining realistic and obtainable goals with our children.

Here are four strategies to help in the acceptance process.

1. Become Educated

The key to your effort is to become familiar with your child's temperament, development, and behavior and use this information proactively in planning parenting practices. By understanding and accepting the unique qualities of each child we can best assist in fostering a resilient mindset.

2. Measure Your Mindset

Honestly consider your reactions in the past to your child's feelings, especially anger. In Step 3 we discussed the importance of empathy in helping children begin to deal with their problems. Make certain that you always begin with empathy.

3. Make Necessary Adjustments
If there is a good match between your expectations and what your children can do, you stand the best chance of helping them deal more constructively with their anger. We don't suggest you give up your dreams and wishes, but realistically understand your children's current state and help them work forward from that point. Thus, we recommend that you separate the dreams you have for your children from who they are as individuals. Be careful not to impose expectations on them based on your needs, interests, or goals.

4. Begin the Process of Collaboration
One of the essential principles of this book is collaboration between you and your children. Once you learn to accept your children for who they are, gain a clearer picture of their unique temperament and style, and begin to make changes in your behavior, it is easier to engage with them in problem-solving discussions of appropriate goals and expectations. When we convey expectations in an accepting, loving, and supportive manner, our children feel motivated to exceed those expectations.

Nurturing Islands of Competence
Coauthor Robert Brooks coined the term *islands of competence* to describe activities that children engage in successfully and from which they experience enhanced self-confidence and esteem. In their books *Raising Resilient Children* and *Nurturing Resilience in Our Children: Answers to the Most Important Parenting Questions*, Drs. Brooks and Goldstein point out that recognizing and celebrating our children's skills and competence nurture a strong, resilient mindset. By assisting your child to develop an island of competence regardless of the skill or ability involved, you strengthen your child's confidence to face challenges, including those posed by intense anger. We must refrain from defining success for our children, but rather encourage them to define their own accomplishments. We must avoid setting the bar too high for them lest we place them in situations that lead to failure and low self-esteem.

We suggest the following five strategies to help your children experience success and to nurture their islands of competence.

1. Openly Enjoy and Celebrate Your Children's Accomplishments
As our children grow they encounter and master innumerable challenges. Although these may seem like small steps to us, to children they represent major advances. Each mastery brings with it a sense of success and achievement, strengthening your child's resolve to deal with new challenges. Children will feel more successful and supported when their achievements are acknowledged and appreciated.

2. Emphasize Your Children's Input in Creating Success
Children and adolescents capable of accepting ownership for their successes will develop high self-esteem. A guiding principle must be to provide experiences and offer comments that convey to your children that they are active participants in what transpires in their lives. This is particularly important in shaping your child's mindset and perception of his ability to manage feelings, including anger. As we do so, we perform a balancing act—namely, being available to assist our children but not doing everything for them.

3. Identify and Reinforce Your Children's Islands of Competence
It is important for you to identify and reinforce these islands and appreciate that they may differ from one child to the next. If we want children to overcome a defeatist mindset we must help them develop self-worth and confidence through successful experiences. Remember also that children will feel greater ownership for their success when they experience these as meaningful to their lives.

4. Give Strengths Time to Develop
Many children require time to develop and mature. If your child demonstrates an interest in a particular activity, even if her skills are below average compared to others, support and nurture the development of her skills within reason. We can never be certain which skills will someday

become a child's islands of competence, reinforcing a sense of success and, most important, a resilient mindset.

5. Accept the Unique Strengths and Successes of Each Child
Children are aware of our disappointment when they don't meet our expectations and are particularly sensitive when their successes are not viewed as important or relevant by parents. We must, through our words and actions, communicate to our children that we accept them and believe in their capabilities. It is impossible to conceive of children developing a resilient mindset or, for that matter, managing anger constructively, if they do not experience the joy and excitement of success in areas that they and significant others in their lives deem to be important.

Learning from Mistakes

The ways in which a child understands and responds to mistakes is an integral feature of a resilient mindset. Some children, when faced with mistakes, are motivated to succeed. Others appear defeated. Some children develop a negative view of mistakes, resorting to counterproductive coping strategies such as avoidance, denial, or anger. Thus, they may not only be angry because they have failed to succeed at a task, but they may also display anger as a means of running from a situation in which they believe they will fail.

As we have noted, there are children who are vulnerable to develop this negative pattern from birth because of their temperament. That is, they appear to come into the world more likely to interpret mistakes as a sign of inadequacy. However, this biological predisposition can be reinforced by the negative comments of parents, excessive expectations, and repeated failure.

Following are four strategies you can use to help your children become increasingly comfortable with the role mistakes play in life. By helping children view mistakes as temporary setbacks and opportunities for learning rather than as indictments of their abilities, we assist them in developing a resilient mindset.

1. Serve As a Model for Dealing with Mistakes and Setbacks

We are the primary models for our children. Our words and actions in response to life's daily challenges affect our children. If children witness parents backing away from challenges and quitting at tasks, they shouldn't be surprised when their children follow the same course of action. Children may not always do what we say, but they often do what we do.

2. Set Realistic Expectations

In our well-intentioned efforts to help our children, we often set the bar too high. By expecting more from children than they are capable of giving, we rob them of the opportunity of learning to view mistakes as challenges. Instead we create a climate in which children retreat from mistakes, frequently feeling frustrated and angry.

3. In Different Ways, Emphasize That Mistakes Are Accepted and Expected

We must communicate that mistakes are a natural part of life. It is important to develop a positive, less defeatist attitude toward mistakes. If you or your child spill something or forget something, remain calm. Verbalize what you or your child might do to lessen the probability of making the same mistake again, and use humor when possible.

4. Love Unconditionally

Many children believe they are accepted and loved only when they do not make mistakes and fail. Often this belief is intensified when parents hold expectations for their children that children cannot meet. This is particularly problematic for children who worry or are sad or angry. Unconditional love remains an underlying principle for helping our children learn to deal with mistakes and perceived failure. It is when our children make mistakes and experience setbacks that our ability to be empathic is truly tested. Children can deal more effectively with frustration and anger if they are not burdened by the fear of mistakes and failures.

Developing Responsibility, Compassion, and a Social Conscience

Young children are strongly motivated to be helpful. Yet many parents tell us that their children have lost this drive by their middle childhood years. They appear to resist many opportunities to be of assistance unless there is something in it for them. In order for a pattern of helpful behavior to emerge and be maintained, parents must nurture this quality, shaping what may well be an inborn trait into a sense of responsibility, compassion, and social conscience. Here are four strategies to assist you in this important task.

1. Serve As a Model of Responsibility
As we have discussed before, when we act responsibly and meet our commitments it increases the likelihood our children will behave in a similar way.

2. Provide Opportunities for Children to Feel They Are Helping Others
Develop traditions to become a charitable family. A charitable family develops a tradition of involving the entire family in helping others. In doing so you are reinforcing in your children the belief that they are important, they are capable of helping others, they are appreciated, and they can make a difference in their world. The more children help others, the less likely they are to be angry.

3. Distribute Responsibilities Evenly Among Family Members
It is important for everyone in the family to understand that they each must make a contribution to the daily life of the family.

4. Take a Helicopter View of Your Child's Life

A helicopter view helps to offset the narrow view we assume sometimes in which we place too much weight on one particular area and ignore others. Thus, we may believe that our children are not responsible if they fail to meet a particular task, but in the process we neglect to take into account the many ways they are helping. A helicopter view will challenge you to observe your child's life from a broader perspective. It may also allow you to gain a more realistic picture of your child's many strengths and the ways in which your child is truly contributing to the household and to others.

Summary

We believe that a resilient mindset is essential for all children, but in particular for children who face adversity in their lives. For those children who struggle with anger, the development of a resilient mindset is very important. Resilience conveys a sense of optimism, ownership, and personal control. It lessens intense anger. Parents can serve as charismatic adults in the lives of their children by believing in them and providing them with opportunities that reinforce their islands of competence and feelings of self-worth.

Conclusion

Anger is a normal human emotion, but it appears frequently to be a unwanted companion when stress, worry, and unhappiness confront children and adolescents. For some children, as you have learned, anger is a highly charged emotion that becomes a primary catalyst for many maladaptive thoughts and behaviors. All families are likely to encounter anger-related issues at some point. Even in the best-functioning families, children may be angry at times at parents. Parents may be angry at children, and children may experience anger regarding other issues or people outside of the home. As you have read, the real issue is how we learn to deal with angry feelings.

In this book you have learned much about the nature of anger and how to help your children develop stress hardiness and resilient skills to cope with anger. We have attempted to provide a model to help you determine when anger becomes a problem and when professional help is required. Developing strategies to help your children learn to manage anger is not a luxury but a necessity for all. After reading this book, it is our hope that you have developed a better understanding of parents' role in this process. You should now possess a set of ideas and strategies and a mindset to help your children.

Let's return to Mulberry Street. In the Kennedy household, Michael, with his parents' guidance, has learned a number of strategies to use when he begins to feel stressed and angry. In the face of frustration, rather than strike out or engage in destructive behavior Michael takes a self-imposed timeout, considers three options to the problem he is facing, chooses one, gains control, and puts it into practice.

In the Reese family, Ellen has begun working with a counselor to focus on developing assertiveness and worry management skills. Ellen's parents have received a number of resources concerning anxiety and depression in childhood. In particular, the Reeses are helping Ellen identify a number of activities that can be used as islands of competence to help her feel successful.

The Juarez parents have learned more about worry in teenagers as well as the role anger plays as a distracting emotion when some people worry. They have helped Janet identify a number of thought-stopping techniques so that she can redirect her thoughts when she feels overwhelmed by fear. As Janet has become more successful with this strategy, the incidence of angry outbursts has been reduced.

The Eskens have completed a thorough learning and psychological evaluation with their daughter, Michelle. Michelle's learning disabilities have been well defined and the Eskens have resources concerning learning problems and strategies for Michelle's difficulties. The Eskens have recognized that punishment is not an effective intervention when children truly struggle to learn. They have modified their parenting strategies and have committed to working cooperatively with Michelle. At the advice of her tutor, they have started a large reading chart to track Michelle's progress so that she can begin to focus on her accomplishments rather than failures.

Richard Smith's father is still struggling with chronic illness. Richard has begun working with a counselor to help him cope with his fears and worries about his father's illness and the family's future. As counseling has begun, Richard has learned a number of different strategies to express his worries, leading to a reduction in angry behavior.

Mr. and Mrs. Schwartz realized that they were and had been modeling behavior they observed in their children. Together the Schwartzes have been working with a marital therapist to develop more effective communication and conflict resolution skills. They have set some clear limits at home about how family members will treat each other.

Finally, despite being suspended from school, seven-year-old Travis has continued to demonstrate aggressive, angry behavior in the face of frustration. Evaluation by the school team raised questions about Travis's learning skills and developing self-discipline. His difficulty sustaining attention, sitting still, and acting impulsively raised the possibility that he may experience attention deficit hyperactivity disorder. The family is in the process of completing further assessment. In the interim, Travis has begun working with the school psychologist, focusing on the skill-building program directed at helping him learn more effective prosocial behaviors in the face of frustration.

We are confident and hopeful that this book has given you the guidance, assistance, and important information you need to work with your child and develop helpful interventions together. We know this program will make a positive difference in your child's life and the life of your family.

Resources

Anxiety

Goldstein, S., K. Hagar, & R. Brooks. 2001. *Seven Steps to Help Your Child Worry Less.* Plantation, FL: Specialty Press.

Hallowell, E. 1998. *Worry: Hope and Help for a Common Condition.* New York: Ballantine Books.

Rapee, R. M., Spence, S. & Wignall, A. 2000. *Helping Your Anxious Child: A Step-by-Step Guide for Parents.* Champaign, IL: New Harbinger.

Attention Deficit Hyperactivity Disorder

Barkley, R. A. 2001. *Taking Charge of ADHD: The Complete, Authoritative Guide for Parents (2nd edition).* New York: Guilford Press.

Dendy, C. Z. 2003. *Teenagers with Attention Deficit (2nd edition).* Bethesda, MD: Woodbine House.

Fowler, M. 2001. *Maybe You Know My Teen.* New York: Broadway Books.

Goldstein, S., & M. Goldstein. 1992. *Hyperactivity: Why Won't My Child Pay Attention?* New York: Wiley.

Hallowell, E. M., & J. J. Ratey. 1994. *Driven to Distraction.* New York: Pantheon Press.

Ingersoll, B. 1998. *Daredevils and Daydreamers: New Perspectives on ADHD*. New York: Doubleday.

Jones, C. 1994. *ADD: Strategies for School Age Children*. San Antonio: Communication Skill Builders.

Jones, C. B. 1991. *Sourcebook on Attention Disorders: A Management Guide for Early Childhood Professionals and Parents*. San Antonio: Communication Skill Builders.

Kilcarr, P. J., & P. O. Quinn. 1997. *Voices from Fatherhood*. New York: Bruner-Mazel.

Parker, H. C. 1992. *The ADD Hyperactivity Handbook for Schools*. Plantation, FL: Specialty Press.

Rief, S. F. 1998. *The ADD/ADHD Checklist: An Easy Reference for Parents and Teachers*. New York: Simon and Schuster.

Rief, S. F., & J. A. Heimburge. 1998. *How to Reach and Teach All Students in the Inclusive Classroom: Ready-to-Use Strategies, Lessons and Activities for Teaching Students with Diverse Learning Needs*. The Center for Applied Research in Education. New York: Jossey-Bass.

Behavioral Problems

Barkley, R. 1998. *Your Defiant Child: Eight Steps to Better Behavior.* New York: Guilford.

Brown, S. 2003. *How to Negotiate with Kids . . . Even When You Think You Shouldn't.* New York: Viking Press.

Clark, L. 1996. *SOS: Help for Parents (2nd edition)*. Bowling Green, KY: Parents Press.

Feindler, E. L., & M. Scalley. 1999. "Adolescent anger-management groups for violence reduction." In T. Kratochwill & K. Stoiber (eds.), *Handbook of Group Interventions for Children and Families*, 100-19. New York: Allyn & Bacon.

Goldstein, A. P., B. Glick, & J. C. Gibbs. 1998. *Aggression Replacement Training: A Comprehensive Intervention for Aggressive Youth.* Champaign, IL: Research Press.

Greene, R. W. 1998. *The Explosive Child: A New Approach for Understanding and Parenting Easily Frustrated, Chronically Inflexible Children.* New York: HarperCollins.

Hammond, W. R. 1991. *Dealing with Anger: A Violence Prevention Program for African-American Youth.* Champaign, IL: Research Press.

Heininger, J., & S. K. Weiss. 2001. *From Chaos to Calm: Effective Parenting of Challenging Children with ADHD and Other Behavioral Problems.* New York: Perigree Books.

Kellner, M. H. 2001. *In Control: A Skill Building Program for Teaching Young Adolescents to Manage Anger.* Champaign, IL: Research Press.

Lavoie, R. 1997. *Learning Disabilities and Discipline: When the Chips Are Down.* Produced by PBS Video, 1320 Braddock Place, Alexandria, VA 22314-1698.

Levy, R., B. O'Hanlon, & T. N. Goode. 2001. *Try and Make Me! Simple Strategies That Turn Off the Tantrums and Create Cooperation.* Emmaus, PA: Rodale Reach.

Murphy, T. 2001. *The Angry Child: Regaining Control When Your Child is Out of Control.* New York: Three Rivers Press.

Phelan, T. W. 1998. *1-2-3 Magic: Effective Discipline for Children 2-12 (2nd edition).* Glen Ellyn, IL: Child Management Press.

Phelan, T. W. 1998. *Surviving Your Adolescents: How to Manage and Let Go of Your 13-18 Year Olds.* Glen Ellyn, IL: Child Management Press.

Robin, A., & S. Foster. 1989. *Negotiating Parent and Adolescent Conflict.* New York: Guilford Press.

Depression

Clark, L. 1998. *SOS Help for Emotions: Managing Anxiety, Anger and Depression.* Bowling Green, KY: Parents Press.

Ingersoll, B. D., & S. Goldstein. 2001. *Lonely, Sad and Angry: A Parent's Guide to Childhood Depression.* Plantation, FL: Specialty Press.

Learning Disability and School Problems

Brooks, R. 1991. *The Self-Esteem Teacher.* Loveland, OH: Treehaus Communications.

Dendy, C. 2000. *Teaching Teens with ADD and ADHD.* Bethesda, MD: Woodbine House.

Goldstein, S., & N. Mather. 1998. *Overcoming Underachieving: An Action Guide to Helping Your Child Succeed in School.* New York: Wiley.

Ingersoll, B., & S. Goldstein. 1993. *Attention Deficit Disorder and Learning Disabilities: Realities, Myths and Controversial Treatments.* New York: Doubleday.

Levine, M. D. 2002. *A Mind at a Time.* New York: Simon and Schuster.

Levine, M. D. 1998. *Educational Care: A System for Understanding and Helping Children with Learning Problems at Home and in School.* Cambridge, MA: Educators Publishing Service.

Levine, M. D. 1996. *Keeping a Head in School.* New York: Educators Publishing Services.

Levine, M. D. 1992. *All Kinds of Minds.* New York: Educators Publishing Services.

Mather, N., & S. Goldstein. 2001. *Learning Disabilities and Challenging Behaviors: A Guide to Intervention and Classroom Management.* Baltimore, MD: Brookes Publishing.

Strick, L., & C. Smith. 1999. *Learning Disabilities A to Z: A Parents' Complete Guide.* New York: Simon and Schuster.

Zentall, S., & S. Goldstein. 1998. *Seven Steps to Homework Success: A Family Guide for Solving Common Homework Problems.* Plantation, FL: Specialty Press.

Online Resources

Anxiety Disorders Association of America
www.adaa.org
Resources on various forms of anxiety conditions

Robert Brooks, Ph.D.
www.drrobertbrooks.com
Articles and resources about raising stress-hardy children

Children and Adults with Attention-Deficit/Hyperactivity Disorder
www.chadd.org
Articles and resources about ADHD across the lifespan

Sam Goldstein, Ph.D.
www.samgoldstein.com
Articles and resources about childhood and adult conditions

Learning Disabilities Association of America
www.ldanatl.org
Articles and resources about learning disabilities across the lifespan

National Adult Literacy and Learning Disabilities Center
www.novel.nifl.gov
Publications, hot topics, and links about learning disabilities and adult
literacy

National Center for Learning Disabilities
www.ncld.org
Information on all aspects of learning disabilities, as well as resources
and links

National Information Center for Children and Youth with Disabilities
www.kidsource.com/NICHCY
Information on all disabilities and related issues

Raising Resilient Children
www.raisingresilientkids.com
Learn more about resilience

Problem Solving

Shure, M. 2000. *Raising a Thinking Preteen.* New York: Henry Holt.

Shure, M. 1994. *Raising a Thinking Child.* New York: Henry Holt.
Shure, M. 1992. *I Can Problem Solve.* New York: Henry Holt.

Resilience

Brazelton, T. B., & S. I. Greenspan. 2000. *The Irreducible Needs of Children: What Every Child Must Have to Grow, Learn and Flourish.* Cambridge, MA: Perseus Publishing.

Brooks, R., & S. Goldstein. 2003. *Nurturing Resilience in Our Children: Answers to the Most Common Parenting Questions.* Chicago: Contemporary Books/McGraw-Hill.

Brooks, R., & S. Goldstein. 2001. *Raising Resilient Children.* Chicago: Contemporary Books/McGraw-Hill.

Goldstein, S., & R. Brooks. 2002. *Raising Resilient Children: A Nine Session Parenting Curriculum to Foster Strength, Hope and Resilience.* Baltimore: Brookes Publishing.

Greenspan, S., & N. B. Lewis. 1999. *Building Healthy Minds: The Six Experiences That Create Intelligence and Emotional Growth in Babies and Young Children.* Cambridge, MA: Perseus Publishing.

Hallowell, E. 1996. *When You Worry About the Child You Love: Emotional and Learning Problems in Children.* New York: Simon and Schuster.

Katz, M. 1997. On *Playing a Poor Hand Well—Insights from the Lives of Those Who Have Overcome Childhood Risks and Adversities.* Chicago: W. W. Norton.

Werner, E., & S. Smith. 2001. *Journeys from Childhood to Midlife: Risk, Resilience and Recovery.* Ithaca, NY: Cornell University Press.

Werner, E., & S. Smith. 1994. *Overcoming the Odds: High Risk Children from Birth to Adulthood.* Ithaca, NY: Cornell University Press.

Addendum 1

Using the Seven-Step Model
As an Adjunct to Treatment

A Guide for Medical and
Mental Health Professionals:

From: *Angry Children, Worried Parents: Seven Steps to Help Families
Manage Anger* by S. Goldstein, R. Brooks, and S. Weiss
(Specialty Press, 2004).
Limited copies may be made for personal use.

Ineffective anger management probably represents one of the most
frequently occurring symptomatic problems when children are referred to
mental health centers or receive mental health services. Although the current
Diagnostic and Statistical Manual of the American Psychiatric Association
does not specifically include an "anger diagnosis of childhood," anger is a
symptom as well as a consequence of the majority of disruptive and
nondisruptive psychiatric problems in children. Acting in spiteful, angry,
and vindictive ways are among the symptoms listed for oppositional defiant
disorder. Youth with conduct disorder are often described as angry.
Typically anger is used to explain the patterns of antisocial behavior these
children exhibit. Although anger is not a symptom of attention deficit
hyperactivity disorder, it is typically one of the most frequent complaints
of parents whose children are referred for ADHD. This may be due in part
to the child's limited capacity to manage frustration and high intensity of
reaction, but also to the high rate of comorbidity between ADHD and other
disruptive psychiatric conditions. Ingersoll and Goldstein (2001) described
depressed youth as "lonely, sad and angry."

When left untreated, depressed youth often progress through periods
of loneliness and sadness, eventually resorting to anger as a means of ex-

119

pressing their unhappiness. Parents frequently report that anxious children resort to anger as stress builds, particularly within the home setting; they lack effective coping strategies to manage worry and daily stress. Many children with learning disability often become frustrated in response to their inability to succeed within an academic setting. Some of these children act out, while others withdraw, but anger is frequently reported among both groups.

Experiencing anger, even high rates of anger, may not necessarily be a problem in and of itself. The problem occurs when children lack effective strategies to cope with and respond appropriately to anger and when adults fail to provide children with the support and care necessary to reduce feelings of anger and develop effective anger management skills.

Students in mental health programs, regardless of discipline, typically are not offered a class in anger or specific training relative to anger management. Most clinical training for mental health professionals focuses on understanding "psychopathology," applying diagnostic principles reliably and validly, and offering one model or another of psychotherapy. Nonetheless, many models of psychotherapy, particularly those with a cognitive orientation, such as rational emotive therapy (Ellis 1962), represent a significant part of the framework of our seven-step anger management model.

What Is Anger?

Anger is a natural human emotion; all people feel and express it at some level. It is but one of many responses individuals express, typically when prevented from reaching their goals. There is nothing wrong with feeling angry in response to a frustrating situation; problems occur when anger leads (consciously or unconsciously) to inappropriate actions or behavior, particularly aggression. Genetics likely contribute significantly to how anger is experienced, expressed, and discharged over time. One's environment likely plays an equal role in the early years within the home and in the later years in the models of peers and other adults.

Anger is typically experienced not just as a psychic phenomena but as a physical response, causing adrenaline to rush through the body and leading some to excessive agitation. In response, some people yell. They become cynical or strike out with aggression. Managing and discharging anger is easier for some than for others, but learning to control anger comes from experience, not genetics. It is a skill that can be modeled and taught to anyone.

Anger may be best conceptualized as a signal, an indication to an individual that a goal or outcome is being blocked and that frustration is building. How people learn to respond to this signal ultimately determines whether they manage anger or anger manages them. In response to anger, some blame others for their problems, using anger as fuel to drive and justify what they view as a necessary response. In our seven-step model, parents teach children that anger is a signal to take effective action rather than a sign of being treated unfairly or a justification for acting inappropriately.

Anger begins as an emotion of varying intensity. It can be experienced as a mild irritation or seemingly unbearable frustration. At the extreme, particularly for children with patterns of impulsive or rigid behavior, anger often leads to intense fury and rage. Physical and biological changes occur in the body. Heart rate and blood pressure increase. Levels of certain hormones, such as adrenaline, increase, leading to other physical changes in the body. Some researchers have suggested that aggression in response to anger may be instinctual. If so, anger may be a natural adaptive response to stress, allowing people to respond to a perceived threat and defend themselves. We suggest that anger not be labeled as a "bad emotion" within the course of psychotherapy. Even in our complex civilized society, a certain level of anger is necessary for survival. However, when angry feelings are generated over minor events or reach excessive proportions, anger becomes a liability.

Webster's New World Dictionary defines anger as "a feeling of displeasure resulting from injury, mistreatment, or opposition, usually manifesting itself in a desire to strike out at the supposed cause of the feeling." Anger can be caused by external or internal events. People can become angry at other individuals, objects, or a particular situation. In extreme cases people can become angry about their own inaccurate perceptions of events that have occurred in their lives. Some children possessing very low emotional thresholds and high intensity of reactions become angry over daily events that rarely cause emotional discomfort for others. Conflicts with peers and siblings cause children to become angry over issues ranging from seating in the car to standing in line at school. Anger is a normal response to physical assault, verbal taunting, or teasing. In some cases, children become angry when they are ignored or restricted from activities. Finally, many children become angry when they "can't do what they want." Children with psychiatric and emotional problems are much more prone to become angry and less likely to possess effective coping skills to deal with anger.

Anger may build in three steps. In the first step, anger represents a sense of arousal, usually occurring when the achievement of a goal is prevented or fulfillment of a need is blocked. In the second step, children externalize their feelings through behavior or verbalization. This can include a sour face, crying, sulking, a random verbalization to express frustration, or a physical or verbal attack on the source of the frustrating experience. It doesn't matter whether the frustrating experience is a sibling or a model airplane; the outcome is the same. Thus, a child may become angry and kick his bicycle when he falls off or become angry at a friend who won't behave in a certain way. When anger progresses to aggressive physical or verbal responses, particularly in situations in which children seek revenge as a means of retaliation, problems usually escalate.

In the third step of anger, the environment then responds to the child. If the child learns that an angry, aggressive response achieves a desired goal, that behavior will be reinforced. Strength of the child's aggressive behavior may be directly related to the level of the aftershock. That is, the way children are responded to either helps them gain better control over anger and develop effective coping strategies or fuels other problems in response to punitive, angry responses from adults. Many children experience punishment or other forms of parental response to their anger that do little to provide them with the tools and skills necessary to respond to frustrating life events more effectively.

Anger As a Catalyst for Aggression

Aggression appears to be a significant consequence of anger. In their book *Frustration and Aggression*, Dollard, Doob, Miller, Mowrer, and Sears (1939) suggested that emotional arousal is influenced by externally driven events. Preventing individuals from reaching their goals leads to frustration, anger, and ultimately aggression. Certainly there are other outcomes for anger besides aggressive behavior. Even within the conceptualization of aggression there may be different types. Some aggression is clearly hostile, designed to inflict harm on others in response to anger. Other aggression may be motivated by secondary gain, predatory in nature. This type of aggression is often referred to as *instrumental.*

Dodge (1991) suggested that acts of aggression that are driven by anger and emotionality reflect *reactive* processes, and those that are predatory in nature reflect *proactive* processes. Some theorists have suggested that there are distinct differences in the behavior and outcome for youth exhibiting these two types of aggressive behavior. The latter are much more often bullies. Children who are reactively aggressive appear to have low emotional thresholds and high intensity of reactions. That is, mildly stressful events induce frustration and anger that leads to aggressive behavior at the slightest provocation by others. There is likely a strong genetic basis for this pattern.

Nearly fifty years ago, Bandura and Walters (1959) suggested that aggressive behavior was learned and governable, not necessarily a genetically endowed, inborn process incapable of modification. Increasingly, however, genetics research is demonstrating that a significant percentage of the variance in when and how people discharge their anger may well be attributed to a combination of genes. Nonetheless, as Bandura pointed out in 1973, it is still believed that human beings are "thinking organisms," which allows them to self-direct behavior (in contrast with animals, which tend to be response oriented). As Larson and Lochman (2002) point out, the intellectual capabilities of human beings allow them to think about their behavior, to consider new behaviors, to evaluate consequences of future behavior, and to learn by watching others. This pattern of observational learning has long been considered an explanation for the means by which children learn to manage anger.

It should also be noted that a response to anger is the result of direct experience. Children reared in environments that do not offer opportunities to learn to manage anger, stress, and frustration, such as settings in which inappropriate coping strategies for these phenomena are commonly exhibited, will likely mirror their experiences in future behavior. The issue of direct experience is further influenced by the biological differences between children. Some children come into the world with problems with self-regulatory skills, making them prone to overreact to minor stresses, to act without thinking, to struggle to consider alternatives in the face of behavior, and, most important, to think ahead and consider the consequences of their future actions. Given these phenomena it is not surprising that children with diagnoses of attention deficit hyperactivity disorder , due to their problems with self-regulation, often struggle to develop effective anger management skills. It is also not surprising that youth with other mental health issues ranging from depression and anxiety to oppositional defiance and conduct disorder also manifest excessive anger and, frequently, adverse coping strategies.

Aggressive behavior in children has been demonstrated to be related to high levels of anger (Eisenberg, Fabes, Nyman, Bernzweig, and Pinuelas, 1994). This pattern is likely further fueled by the child's inability to regulate emotion in response to anger-producing events (Lochman, Dunn, and Wagner, 1997). These authors suggested that individuals may exhibit two types of anger, provoked and unprovoked. They point out that when an individual perceives threat (that is, the individual is provoked) the response can be a deliberate, calculated anger. Stimulation of the adreno-hypothalamic-cortico hormonal system of the brain creates a state of readiness, but also agitation. This pattern of activation is stimulated by a variety of stressors. Individuals more sensitive to this reaction, such as those experiencing depression or attention-deficit/hyperactivity disorder, produce high levels of intense anger in response to minor stress. As Goleman (1995) points out, anger can fuel further anger, leading to an escalating pattern of inappropriate behavior. For some individuals, anger develops very rapidly due to biological differences in the brain, particularly in the limbic system, as well as inefficiencies in the regulation of the heart by the vagus nerve (Porges 1995). For example, boys with high rates of aggression in response to frustration and anger have lower resting heart rates but display a sharp surge in heart rate that represents release of vagus nerve control of the heart in the face of conflict (Craven 1996).

Our seven-step anger management model is based on a cognitive behavioral framework and the tenets of social information processing. The six cognitive operations that appear to explain why some children cope adequately with anger and others do not reflect the six steps that children need to enact for competent social problem solving in the face of anger. The model, developed by Crick and Dodge (1994), is as follows:

Step 1: Encoding
>An event takes place and a child gathers information through
>the various senses by observation and interaction.

Step 2: Representation and Interpretation
>By thinking, the child seeks understanding and meaning of the
>behavior he is observing.

Step 3: Goal Selection
> The child decides the ultimate goal of a response to the behavior observed.

Step 4: Response Access
> The child considers a variety of alternatives, weighing the relative benefits and liabilities of each.

Step 5: Decision Process
> By considering the risks and benefits, the child decides which alternative is the best.

Step 6: Behavioral Enactment
> Once a response is chosen, the child sets it into motion.

Aggression in response to anger has also been conceptualized within an information-processing model. Many of the research-proven interventions for disruptive behavior are based on cognitive behavioral theories. Cognitions, or thoughts, influence behavior. By altering the cognitions children use to interpret the behavior of others, at-risk youth can alter their behavior. As some researchers have conceptualized, it is not necessarily a frustrating or stressful event that provokes anger but rather the child's thinking about that event and failing to develop an appropriate repertoire of responses (Lochman, Nelson, and Sims, 1981). Based on this theoretical model, Lochman, Lampron, Gemmer, Harris, and Wyckoff (1989) developed the Anger Control Program. They refined this program in a recent text directed at group-based school intervention to facilitate anger management and reduction of aggression in conflict situations (Larson and Lochman 2002). Mental health professionals considering small group intervention for anger management are encouraged to consider this model.

Anger As a Consequence of Coercive Family Processes

In 1982, Gerald Patterson offered the term *coercive family process* to describe a pattern of behavior within families in which ineffective parent management fueled an escalating pattern of child behavior problems, which then fueled further ineffective parental actions. Patterson demonstrated that this process increased rather than decreased inappropriate responses to anger, including aggression and noncompliance. In this process, the effectiveness with which parents manage inappropriate child behavior plays a pivotal role in determining the child's future behavior; in this case, capacity to cope with stress, frustration, and anger. This pattern of family interaction can usually be elicited during a history-taking session or family interview. When mental health professionals identify the pattern, parents will require supportive, professional assistance beyond just the seven-step model in order to break these processes and develop adaptive parenting behaviors.

Some children appear by virtue of their natural temperament to be more prone to fuel this pattern of behavior in parents. In these families, ineffective parenting practices reinforce noncompliant, angry, and coercive child behavior multiple times each day. When parents seek compliance, children quickly resort to escape ("I won't do it!"), often manifested through angry, verbally aggressive behaviors. Out of frustration and desire for harmony, parents give in. This then reinforces the child's behavior, in particular the use of angry expressions to respond to undesirable requests. It is important for mental health professionals to recognize that in these situations parents possess a very narrow repertoire of discipline strategies, frequently limited to verbal or physical aggression, which models the very angry outbursts they seek to extinguish in their children.

Evaluating Anger

If, within the context of therapeutic treatment, a plan to help children reduce anger and learn to manage anger is not created, treatment success will likely be compromised, particularly when anger is a prevalent, potent symptom. Although medications may reduce the incidence of angry outbursts in some children, they tend not to reduce how children respond to anger. Pills are no substitute for skills. Thus, no matter what the condition or problem, assessing the nature of angry behavior in children referred for therapeutic consideration is a key component of any psychological, psychiatric, or social work evaluation.

An anger assessment component evaluation should focus on anger issues and include queries about the following:
- Experiences that make the child angry
- Number of times a week the child becomes angry
- Intensity and strength of anger
- How long it takes the child to recover
- What behaviors consistently precede angry outbursts

- The consequences of the child's anger within the family and between family members
- Which strategies have been attempted successfully and unsuccessfully
- Evaluation of factors that might contribute to anger, including poor impulse control in the child, neurodevelopmental problems, anxiety, depression, frustration, or family circumstances

Incorporating Anger Management Strategies into Parent Consultation

Miller (1994) outlined six critical parental competencies necessary to help parents intervene effectively with angry children.

1. Tracking, labeling and pinpointing. Learn to effectively monitor your child's behavior to avoid falling back on generalizations and to develop an understanding of the events that precede and follow inappropriate angry outbursts.

2. Emphasize positive behavior in your child, recognizing and reinforcing appropriate behavior when it occurs.

3. Give appropriate commands and avoid ambiguous communication. Understand the difference between *alpha* (clear) and *beta* (unclear) commands, as well as the *start* and *stop* variety of each. Beta commands, because they are ambiguous, are rarely effective. "Don't do it" is an example of a stop beta command; "Do it" is a start beta command. In neither scenario does the child have a clear understanding of what it is she is to do or not to do. Stop commands are generally ineffective because they leave a range of other inappropriate behaviors available to the child. For example, a child may stop hitting his brother but then begin kicking. Even a stop alpha command (for example, "Stop hitting your brother!") does not provide the child with a directed behavior. Start alpha commands, however, avoid these pitfalls. Directing a child hitting her brother to place her hands in her pockets and her feet on the floor lets the child know exactly what you want her to do rather than what you would like her to stop doing.

4. Develop strategies to engage in nonphysical discipline. Master behavioral interventions, including response cost, timeout, and differential attention.

5. Communicate effectively, listen actively, empathize, and jointly solve problems. Our seven-step anger management model provides parents with a framework to develop and practice these skills.

6. Develop a set of resources and strategies to troubleshoot when specific problems occur, as well as to apply skills used effectively with a particular problem or situation.

Incorporating Anger Management Strategies During the Course of Counseling or Consultation

During parenting consultation, when the discussion turns to anger it is important as a basic foundation to help parents understand the following five keys:

1. Anger is a normal emotion experienced by everyone. The experience of anger is not bad.

2. Anger can be used as a cue to guide effective problem-solving behavior.

3. Anger is one outcome when individuals experience frustration, but not the only one. Thus, children can be taught strategies that will reduce the occurrence of anger.

4. Parents' and children's mindset about anger and the role it plays in everyday life is an important variable in predicting the success of an anger management program.

5. Multiple effective strategies can reduce the experience of anger and lead to effective problem resolution when anger is experienced.

It is beyond the scope of this brief addendum to provide an in-depth anger management program. Many of the strategies and solutions offered within this book can be easily adapted and used during consultation or psychotherapy. Readers interested in in-depth anger management programs should consult additional resources, including the following.

Clark, L. 1998. *SOS Help for Emotions: Managing Anxiety, Anger and Depression.* Bowling Green, KY: Parents Press.

Goldstein, A. P., & E. McGinnis. 1997. *Skillstreaming the Adolescent.* Champaign, IL: Research Press.

Kellner, M. H. 2001. *In Control: A Skill-Building Program for Teaching Young Adolescents to Manage Anger.* Champaign, IL: Research Press.

Larson, J., & J. E. Lochman. 2002. *Helping School Children Cope with Anger: A Cognitive-Behavioral Intervention.* New York: Guilford.

McGinnis, E., & A. P. Goldstein. 2003. *Skillstreaming in Early Childhood (Revised).* Champaign, IL: Research Press.

References

Bandura, A. 1973. *Aggression: A Social Learning Analysis.* Englewood Cliffs, NJ: Prentice-Hall.

Bandura, A., & R. H. Walters. 1959. *Adolescent Aggression.* New York: Ronald Press.

Beck, R., & E. Fernandez. 1998. "Cognitive-behavioral therapy in the treatment of anger: A meta-analysis." *Cognitive Therapy in Research* 22:63-74.

Craven, S. 1996. "Examination of the role of physiological and emotional arousal in reactive aggressive boys' hostile attributional biases in peer provocation situations." Unpublished manuscript. Durham, NC: Duke University.

Crick, N. R., & K. A. Dodge. 1994. "A review and reformulation of social information-processing mechanisms in children's social adjustment." *Psychological Bulletin* 115:74-101.

Deffenbacher, J. L., R. S. Lynch, E. R. Oetting, & C. C. Kemper. 1996. "Anger reduction in early adolescence." *Journal of Counseling Psychology* 43:149-57.

Dodge, K. A. 1991. "The structure and function of reactive and proactive aggression." In D. J. Pepler & K. H. Rubin (eds.), *Development and Treatment of Childhood Aggression*, 201-18. Hillsdale, NJ: Erlbaum.

Dollard, J., L. W. Doob, N. E. Miller, O. H. Mowrer, & R. R. Sears. 1939. *Frustration and Aggression.* New Haven, CT: Yale University Press.

Eisenberg, N., R.A. Fabes, M. Nyman, J. Bernzweig, & A. Pinuelas. 1994. "The relations of emotionality and regulation to children's anger-related reactions." *Child Development* 65:109-28.

Ellis, A. 1962. *Reason and Emotion in Psychotherapy.* New York: Lyle Stuart.

Feindler, E. L., & R. B. Ecton. 1996. *Adolescent Anger Control: Cognitive-Behavioral Techniques.* New York: Pergamon Press.

Goldstein, A. P., B. Glick, & J. C. Gibbs. 1998. *Aggression Replacement Training: A Comprehensive Intervention for Aggressive Youth (Revised).* Champaign, IL: Research Press.

Goleman, D. 1995. *Emotional Intelligence.* New York: Bantam Books.

Ingersoll, B., & S. Goldstein. 2001. *Lonely, Sad and Angry: How to Help Your Unhappy Child.* Plantation, FL: Specialty Press.

Kassinove, H. 1995. *Anger Disorders: Definition, Diagnosis and Treatment.* Washington, DC: Taylor and Francis.

Kellner, M. H. 2001. *In Control: A Skill Building Program for Teaching Young Adolescents to Manage Anger.* Champaign, IL: Research Press.

Kellner, M. H., & J. Tutin. 1995. "A school based anger management program for developmentally and emotionally disabled high school students." *Adolescents* 30:813-42.

Larson, J. & J. E. Lochman. 2002. *Helping School Children Cope with Anger: A Cognitive-Behavioral Intervention.* New York: Guilford.

Lochman, J. E., S. E. Dunn, & E. E. Wagner. 1997. "Anger." In G. Bear, K. Minke, & A. Thomas (eds.), *Children's Needs II*, 149-60. Washington, DC: National Association of School Psychologists.

Lochman, J. E., L. B. Lampron, T. C. Gemmer, S. R. Harris, & G. M. Wyckoff. 1989. "Teacher consultation and cognitive-behavioral interventions with aggressive boys." *Psychology in the Schools* 26:179-88.

Lochman, J. E., W. M. Nelson, & J. P. Sims. 1981. "A cognitive behavioral program for use with aggressive children." *Journal of Clinical Child Psychology 13:146-8.*

Miller, G. 1994. "Enhancing family-based interventions for managing childhood anger and aggression." In M. J. Furlong & D. C. Smith (eds.), *Anger, Hostility, and Aggression: Assessment, Prevention, and Intervention Strategies for Youth*, 83-116. Brandon, VT: Clinical Psychology.

Patterson, G. R. 1982. *Coercive Family Process.* Eugene, OR: Castalia.

Porges, S. W. 1995. "Orienting in a defensive world: Mammalian modifications of our evolutionary heritage. A polyvagal theory." *Psychophysiology* 32:301-18.

Wilcox, D., & B. W. Dowrick. 1992. "Anger management with adolescents." *Residential Treatment for Children and Youth* 9:29-39.

Addendum 2

Helping Children Cope with Anger:
A Guide for Teachers

From: *Angry Children, Worried Parents: Seven Steps to Help Families Manage Anger* by S. Goldstein, R. Brooks, and S. Weiss (Specialty Press, 2004).
Limited copies may be made for personal use.

Children with disruptive behaviors, such as angry physical or verbal outbursts, present some the most difficult challenges facing teachers at all grade levels. These behaviors create a chaotic climate in the classroom and dramatically affect a teacher's availability to other students. This is equally true on the elementary and secondary levels of education. Strong feelings of anger are often evidenced by verbal and/or physical aggression, tantrums, destruction of property, and general noncompliance.

It is unclear why some children are much more likely to act out angry behavior. Some children may come into the world with a biological risk to behave this way. As infants, the smallest frustration provoked tantrums and outbursts in them. As they grew older, they continued to be quick to anger. They often projected the source of their anger onto others and thus seemed uncaring about the feelings of others. Whether or not the student has a learning or attention issue or defined mental health problems that underlie the behaviors, patterns of angry behavior within the classroom have been found to strongly contribute to long-term risk for school failure and later serious maladjustment (Biederman, Mick, Faraone, and Burback 2001).

Implementing strategies to assist students in developing better anger management is essential to help them adopt necessary behavior changes. Understanding anger and providing the structure and supports necessary to address the behaviors that often accompany this emotion are the first steps to helping these students.

This brief guide will focus specifically on strategies to help children learn to manage anger within the school setting. It will not focus on children with defined mental health problems leading to angry behavior at school, such as attention deficit hyperactivity disorder, oppositional defiance, conduct disorder, depression, anxiety, or learning disability. Interested readers should consult Mather and Goldstein (2001) for an in-depth, hands-on guide to strategies to manage a variety of behavioral and emotional problems in regular classroom settings.

What Is Anger?

Anger is a natural human emotion. It is one of many responses individuals can express when they are prevented from reaching their goals. Problems occur when anger leads to inappropriate actions or behavior. The problem, then, is not *being* angry, but learning to deal with angry feelings in an inappropriate way.

Anger can be experienced not just as an emotion but as a physical response, causing adrenaline to rush through our bodies, leading to agitation. Although anger is a natural emotion that we all experience, learning to control it comes from experience, not genetics. It is a skill that can be modeled and taught to children. The interaction of genetics and experience ultimately determines whether children develop adaptive coping strategies to deal with anger or create a pattern of dysfunctional behavior and relationships.

Anger may build in three steps. In the first step, it represents a sense of arousal, usually occurring when the achievement of a goal is prevented or fulfillment of a need is blocked. In the second step, children externalize their feelings through behavior or verbalization. This can include a sour face, crying, sulking, a random verbalization to express frustration, or a physical or verbal attack on the source of the frustrating experience. It doesn't matter whether the frustrating experience is an assignment or playground conflict; the outcome is the same.

In the third step of anger, the environment responds to the child. If the child learns that an angry, aggressive response achieves a desired goal, that behavior will be reinforced. That is, the way children are responded to either helps them gain better control over anger and develop effective coping strategies or leads to an escalation of the same behaviors. Many children experience punishment or other forms of response to their anger that do little to provide them with the tools and skills necessary to respond to frustrating life events more effectively.

When Anger Becomes a Problem

Anger can be caused by external or internal events. In extreme cases people can become angry about their own inaccurate perceptions of events that have occurred in their lives. Some children possessing very low emotional thresholds and high intensity of reactions become angry over daily events that rarely cause emotional discomfort for others. Conflicts with peers cause children to become angry over issues ranging from taking turns to standing in line at school to pairings for cooperative learning assignments. In some cases, children become angry when they are ignored or restricted from activities. Of course all teachers know that children become angry when they "can't do what they want." Anger appears to be a very common response when children feel helpless or hopeless. When anger overcomes us we don't think logically or rationally. Children must learn that anger is a signal to take action rather than a sign of being treated unfairly. How children (or adults, for that matter) learn to respond to this signal will determine whether they manage anger or anger manages them.

Teaching Anger Management

The goal of teaching children anger management is to reduce excessive reactions and help children use anger as a signal to redirect their behavior. As with learning to swim or to ride a bicycle, as you begin to work with a student it is important to keep an open mind. Not all children learn to swim in the first lesson or master riding a bicycle the first day. Some children require much longer periods of practice to develop proficiency.

Keep in mind also that some children are born more likely to be irritable and easily angered or frustrated. These symptoms usually present from an early age. Yet it is also important to keep in mind that some children behave this way because they live in households in which they are exposed to models of poor anger management. Some children experience both risks, leading to a significant probability that they will struggle to learn to manage anger effectively.

Angry outbursts can mark a child for exclusion and alienation by her classmates. An inability to contain anger and deal effectively with the emotion may result in the additional frustration of poor peer relationships. It is, therefore, crucial for educators to understand what can be done to reduce the likelihood that anger may spill over into the educational setting. Often the best offense is the defense that advanced preparation, structure, and new tools and scripts can provide.

Because children struggling with anger are prone to externalize their problems and have little hope that interventions that involve their active participation will be successful, teachers can emphasize that if the first strategy doesn't work, the child can then rely on the second or third strategy. The message to these students should be that anger is a natural feeling but can become a problem if not expressed constructively, that there are steps that can be taken to manage anger more effectively, that some solutions may take time to be successful, and that some may not be effective at all and that others may be attempted. We want to develop realistic optimism and a sense of hope in our children.

Changing Negative Scripts and Mindsets

The success of considering and using new strategies to replace those that have proven ineffective in the past demands that we demonstrate the insight and courage to change our own behaviors so that students might change theirs. To use the same ineffective script repeatedly will guarantee continued frustration and anxiety.

Even the best-intentioned educator may fall into the negative scripts of using a raised voice, telling students what not to do, failing to involve them in the problem-solving process, and becoming frustrated and angry when attempts to ease the problem are unsuccessful. If we remain empathic and remember that students will be more willing to change their behavior when they sense our support and feel they have some control of the situation, then we can more effectively help them handle their frustration and anger; in the process we also nurture their confidence and self-reliance.

The Importance of Perspective

There is little question that anger management is learned. Although neurobiology can have a significant influence, the ability to handle anger effectively is not something we are born with. Many different factors influence our ability to manage anger. Often we lose perspective, reading things into a child's pattern of responses that we should not. Proper perspective is essential to our being able to model good anger management. Consider the following ways you can maintain a proper perspective.

Don't Take Angry Behavior Personally
No child developed a behavior just to get back at you. By the time children reach school age they have been practicing—ask their parents or last year's teachers. The way we interpret a student's behavior factors significantly in how we respond. Do not attribute negative motives to a child's behavior. The moment you do, you will be more reactive than responsive.

Make Sure Your Expectations for Change Are Realistic
Perhaps in the past you have employed excellent interventions that have resulted in positive change. But because your goal was to eliminate a behavior entirely, when it continued to occur, even at lower rates, you stopped what you were doing. A realistic goal of behavior change is that the negative behavior occurs less often, is not as intense, and/or doesn't last as long. Any one of these changes represents progress—it doesn't have to be all of them.

Look for Trends
Don't be defeated by a single incident or bad day. Progress is measured in steps. It doesn't happen all at once and it doesn't happen overnight. Did this week go better than the last? Has the student's ability to handle frustration improved since the start of the school year? Recognize and reinforce improvement when you see it, in whatever form it takes.

Know the Student
Thinking that a student *ought* to be able to or that he *can already* do something he cannot will inevitably lead to frustration and failure. His age may not be a good measure of his ability to handle a series of directions or assignments. Maybe he *should* be able to process a three-part direction or handle a long-term project as his classmates can, but he can't. And thinking he should doesn't make it so.

Consider the Child

What are her individual strengths? What does she do well? What kinds of activities does she enjoy, and are any of these part of the lesson plan? When trying adaptations on the secondary level, take into consideration her favorite classes. Many of the most challenging students have fewer difficulties in classes that interest them. Use a new tool or approach in a high-interest class first so the student and you experience success before trying it in more challenging classes. Before you make changes, you must see this student for what she is instead of what she is not and value and build on her strengths. A realistic view of a student's strengths and "improvables" decreases the likelihood that inflated expectations will result in frustration and anger.

The Power of Reward

The key to real behavior change is identifying and noticing positive behavior. Take the time to notice when a child manages anger effectively. Jump all over it. This is one of the best ways to clarify your expectations for anger management and will be better received than the punishment following an angry outburst. Be prepared: whatever's going right will pass, so give your positive feedback immediately. Some children's performance is so erratic that if an opportunity to reinforce is missed, it may be lost. Leave a note, give a hand signal across the classroom, initial a card every student has taped to his desk, or pair your praise with a privilege or other concrete reinforcer. Kids struggling with anger management are difficult to work with, but the positives can reduce the negatives.

Make Behavior a Priority

If you don't proactively teach appropriate behavior—take time out of your day and schedule it into curriculum time—negative, inappropriate behavior will get your attention and take up your time. Take a moment at the start of class to review behavioral expectations or to set a goal for the day, discuss a guideline, or establish a secret signal—a visual cue to stop or reinforce a behavior. If you don't make behavior a priority it will become one.

Clarify Expectations

All children need limits. Clearly stated guidelines, consistently enforced, give a sense of security and predictability. It is a way for students to know what is expected and what are the consequences of meeting or not meeting those expectations. More often, however, we tell kids what the rules are right after they break them. This leads to a lot of anger and frustration for both teacher and student. We point out each time a student is late for class, but rarely clearly establish a time to be seated and then follow up by reinforcing those sitting quietly at that time. If a student has this information in advance, then the outcome is more the child's choice.

Have older elementary and secondary students identify behaviors and guidelines *they* think are important. Select two or three that are most important. Discuss the rules, ask for definitions, and clarify exactly what is expected. For younger students (kindergarten through 6th grade), provide role play opportunities for each guideline. Students can identify their own behavioral goal of the week and post it on their desks or notebook.

Once the guidelines have been defined, reinforce those who adhere to them. Be specific about what you see that you want to see again. Saying "You got started on your work without a reminder" is much more encouraging than lecturing a student who is chronically slow to begin working. A bonus written at the top of the worksheet right after he begins work acts as an incentive to continue working.

Often the biggest battles are over a clash of expectations. The student enters the situation with her own concept of how or when things occur, and when they don't happen that way behavior escalates. Reviewing what's coming in terms of sequence or structure or what the behavioral expectations are (rather than what is prohibited), defining limits in anticipation of events, is often enough to reduce angry outbursts.

Prioritize: Narrow the Focus

Decide what is most important to work on. You can't work on everything at once. Be specific about expectations and notice improvement. That entails breaking down your expectations into steps a student can achieve. Reinforce progress—take note of improvement rather than waiting for a total turnaround. The student you find most challenging will make progress in steps. There are no overnight successes with behavior.

Include the student in discussions of behavior. Ask each student to identify one behavior he needs to work on. If a child is part of the solution, he feels less the brunt of the problem. When he doesn't feel as if he's a problem, he is less likely to feel angry. Besides, there's a much greater likelihood he'll retain a guideline he helped develop.

Establish Routines

Establishing routines in a classroom, procedures that remain the same every day, is one of the best supports you can give a student. All children need structure in their lives. Some can develop it for themselves, but most—especially challenging ones—need adults to provide that structure for them. Similarly, most kids prefer predictability. For some children, however, predictability isn't merely desirable or preferable—it's essential. The frustration of not knowing what is expected or what's coming next can be the spark for a student who struggles with anger. Without it, she may feel out of control or overwhelmed by the moment. This can easily result in anger. A child who feels out of control might act that way.

Establishing routines and schedules (with input from the child whenever possible) helps to provide that essential predictability. The same routine for taking down and handing in assignments or arriving at school, for example, provide the opportunity to practice and develop efficiency in that pattern of behavior. When students follow the routine, provide reinforcement.

Tools to Help Establish Expectations and Routines

Document as much as possible. Put expectations and routines (outlined in steps) in writing. Use tools that specify expectations in clear, visual terms. Visual cues depersonalize expectations and clarify limits. When you give direction and leave the room, what's left of your direction? Nothing. You reappear and you are the visual cue for the direction. This increases a student's reliance on you to remind him. It makes it necessary for you to keep telling him what is expected and what comes next. It perpetuates that sense that he just can't seem to get it right. The less capable he feels, the angrier he may become.

List task expectations, including interim deadlines for completion. What needs to be done, and by when? Post guidelines and behavioral objectives as well as a record of success. These tools should not only clarify what you want to see, but what will happen when students get it right and when they don't. When you use lists, timers, schedules, and calendars, they remind the child so you don't have to. Remember the formula:

Checklists + Schedules = Predictability = Fewer Angry Meltdowns

By paring down expectations to what is truly essential, putting them into a routine, documenting what you expect with a visual cue, and reinforcing adherence to the routine, things will go more smoothly. Your students rely on the structure that makes their world predictable and thrive on the reinforcement that acknowledges their success.

Consider one aspect of the daily routine and determine whether you have:

- narrowed the focus, making sure expectations are reasonable (Can she do it without you, or does she need a predetermined number of reminders?),
- put expectations in writing so the list becomes the measure of success, not you, and
- provided incentives for completing the tasks successfully.

Pass It On

Try to keep an informal list of strategies that seem to facilitate a child's success. Jot down aspects of classroom structure and techniques that were especially helpful to your students so that this information is available to their future teachers. Doing so spares teachers the job of reinventing the wheel. And it can be so reassuring to the struggling student to begin a new year with some of the same tools and supports. All too often, the most successful approaches are forgotten at the end of the academic year.

Finally, if you have a successful year, consider meeting with next year's staff to share information. Even sharing what has *not* worked is helpful. That way the new teachers know that whatever you suggest has already been tested in the classroom. Teachers are more likely to use strategies that are known to work for a student, especially if they hear it from another teacher.

Anticipate the Ups and Downs

Be prepared for frequent setbacks. When positive change occurs, and it will, rest assured that whatever is going right will not last. The best of behavioral changes, like the worst, invariably pass. If you anticipate the lapses, you'll be less frustrated when they happen. Realistic expectations in terms of the inevitable setbacks reduce anger in both the educator and the child.

Narrow your focus. Define changes in terms of improvement (not perfection). Anticipate the ups and downs. Reinforce any success. All children benefit from praise.

Finally, don't raise the bar too quickly. Once you have achieved some success, savor it. Don't increase your expectations just yet. Allow the child and yourself the opportunity to enjoy the moment. He's not yet proficient at whatever has been achieved. It's still a work in progress.

Incorporating Anger Management Strategies into the Classroom

There are six critical competencies necessary for teachers to intervene effectively with anger problems in the classroom. These six steps are based on the work of Miller (1994).

1. Develop a system to track, label, and pinpoint angry behavior. Such a system will allow teachers to effectively monitor children's behavior, avoid reinforcing angry outbursts, and develop an understanding of the events that precede and follow angry outbursts.

2. Emphasize the positive behavior of your students, recognizing and reinforcing appropriate behavior when it occurs.

3. Give appropriate commands and avoid ambiguous communication. Understand the difference between *alpha* (clear) and *beta* (unclear) commands, as well as the *start* and *stop* variety of each. Beta commands, because they are ambiguous, are rarely effective. "Don't do it" is an example of a stop beta command; "Do it" is a start beta command. In neither scenario does the child have a clear understanding of what it is she

is to do or not to do. Stop commands are generally ineffective because they leave a range of other inappropriate behaviors available to the child. For example, a child may stop hitting his brother but then begin kicking. Even a stop alpha command (for example, "Stop hitting your classmate!") does not provide the child with a directed behavior. Start alpha commands, however, avoid these pitfalls. Directing a child hitting her brother to place her hands in her pockets and her feet on the floor lets the child know exactly what you want her to do rather than what you would like her to stop doing.

4. Master behavioral interventions as described in this guide.

5. Communicate effectively, listen actively, empathize, and jointly solve problems.

6. Develop a set of resources and strategies to troubleshoot when specific problems occur, as well as to apply skills used effectively with a particular problem or situation.

References

Biederman, J., E. Mick, S. V. Faraone, & M. Burback. 2001. "Patterns of remission and symptom decline in conduct disorder: A 4-year prospective study of an ADHD sample." *Journal of the American Academy of Child and Adolescent Psychiatry* 40:290-8.

Mather, N., & Goldstein, S. 2001. *Learning Disabilities and Challenging Behaviors.* Baltimore: Paul H. Brookes Publishers.

Miller, G. 1994. "Enhancing family-based interventions for managing childhood anger and aggression." In M. J. Furlong & D. C. Smith (eds.), *Anger, Hostility, and Aggression: Assessment, Prevention and Intervention Strategies for Youth,* 83-116. Brandon, VT: Clinical Psychology.

Index